later encounters

SEVEN ONE-ACT PLAYS

leonard melfi

WITHDRAWN

SAMUEL FRENCH, INC.

25 WEST 45TH STREET NEW YORK 10036
7623 SUNSET BOULEVARD HOLLYWOOD 90046
LONDON TORONTO

CONTENTS

Taffy's Taxi 9

Tripper's Taxi 29

Toddy's Taxi 41

The Teaser's Taxi 63

Mr. Tucker's Taxi 85

Rusty and Rico 113

Lena and Louie 151

TAXI TALES

(FIVE ONE-ACT PLAYS)

For:

Joe Regan
and
Edward Berkeley

TAXI TALES originated as a workshop project at the Circle In The Square, and was first presented by Joe Regan on December 28th, 1978, at the Century Theatre, New York City, with the following cast:

MANDY, LORNA, JOANNA, LOVELY
MIMI, SISTER SERENA .... *Paula Christopher*

ANDY, LADDIE, TRIPPER, TEASER .... *Al Corley*

TAFFY, GIGI, BETSY .... *Julie DeLaurier*

MOMMY, CONTESSA DRAKE,
MRS. TUCKER .... *Dolly Jonah*

TODDY, SPIKE HORN, LEFTY .... *Ken Olin*

DADDY, SPEED, MR. TUCKER .... *Michael Strong*

Directed by Edward Berkeley

Scenery designed by Hugh Landwehr

Costumes designed by Hilary Rosenfeld

Lighting designed by Arden Fingerhut

Sound designed by Garry Harris

Production Stage Manager: Ellen Raphael

Original song "Taxi" by Jonathan Hogan

Taffy's Taxi

THE PEOPLE OF THE PLAY
(*as they speak*)

TAFFY: a truly tempting-looking woman who is somewhere in her early 30's and who has short-cropped raven-black hair and a deep smooth raven-velvet voice to go with it; she is a New York City taxicab driver, well-built, to put it mildly, who is dressed in a crisp bright yellow mannish shirt that is unbuttoned halfway down and that has a golden heart-shaped pin attached to it on the left side, a pair of nicely-fitting dark blue pants that are held up by a belt made of golden chains, and a small black leather cap on her head; she also smokes a whole lot.

THE FIRST COUPLE: (The Honeymooners):
   ANDY: a good-looking guy in his late 20's.
   MANDY: a good-looking girl in her middle 20's.

THE SECOND COUPLE: (The Swinging Singles):
   LADDIE: a cool-looking young man in his early 20's.
   LORNA: a chic-looking young woman in her late teens.
   JOANNA: a lovely young creature who is exactly 21 years old.

(NOTE: The parts of ANDY, MANDY, LADDIE, LORNA, and JOANNA have been written so that they can all be played by one actor and one actress.)

WHERE THEY ARE

The streets and avenues of Manhattan; telephone booths of Manhattan; and a taxicab of Manhattan.

(NOTE: There is only one setting and it should be filling the whole stage with great unreal immensity. We should have the overall impression that we could almost possibly be inside a very modern museum that is showing the mammoth paintings and gigantic sculptures and sprawling mobiles of a marvelous pop-mad artist who uses the clearest and the brightest colors imaginable. The ACTRESS and the ACTORS never use anything that is real, but with the *very real* exception of TAFFY's chain-smoking. (Her constant cigarette smoke does nice hazy forming as it intermingles with the varied lighting of the play). Everything is done through simple suggestive mime: they all talk and walk and ride and sit and stand amid the blaring-glaring atmosphere of a sad happy dream-nightmare: perhaps an abstract modern Gotham version of what we would think it would be like to be in the uniquely adventurous world of 'Alice-In-Wonderland' today.)

WHEN

From midnight until eight o'clock in the morning during the late winter during the beginning of the late 1970's.

Taffy's Taxi

Before the CURTAIN goes up we hear Roberta Flack's voice which is obviously coming from a jukebox: she is singing: "Feel Like Makin' Love." Then we hear lots of New York City traffic sounds. Eventually they almost all die away into practically nothing as the CURTAIN goes up and the LIGHTS come up while the music continues to play on. We see TAFFY *SEATED at the steering-wheel in the front seat of her taxicab. Occasionally we hear the honk of a lonely horn from some other motor vehicle in the immediate vicinity or far, far away. Presently we can hear an emergency police siren in the definite distance. We notice that* TAFFY *is terribly pensive behind the wheel. She begins to sing the song with Roberta Flack. Then, almost without thinking, she stops her empty taxicab and jumps out of it. She goes to a telephone booth and dials a number.*

TAFFY (*Into the mouthpiece nervously*) It's me, darling. How are you? Oh . . . ? Well, I'm sorry. I really and truly am, but . . . well, I just said I was sorry, didn't I? Oh, no! Please don't! No, don't! Don't hang up, please?! I am really and truly very sorry that I woke you up. I really am, darling. Oh, please, honey: just let me finish, will you . . . please?! It's just that, no matter what, well, you know that it's just about totally impossible for me *not* to be thinking about all of the goddam gorgeous time, no matter what time of day or night it is whenever I'm not with you and you're not with me, whenever I can't see you, whenever I can't hear you, whenever I can't touch you, whenever I can't smell you . . . no, no, NO! Please let me finish darling! *Whenever I can't taste you!* No, sweetheart, please, no: *don't hang up!*
> (*We hear an extremely loud replica of a telephone being abruptly hung-up: it should be as though it is coming over a "bigger-than-life" public address system.* TAFFY *is more nervous than ever now. Very quietly she places the telephone receiver back upon its hook, and then she takes out a cigarette and lights it. She does this throughout the rest of the play. Roberta Flack has just stopped singing*)

(*The* FIRST COUPLE *enter;* ANDY *and* MANDY)

ANDY Taxi?!

TAFFY Yes . . .

ANDY The Hilton!

TAFFY Which one?
(ANDY *and* MANDY *climb into the back seat of the taxicab*)

ANDY Oh? Well . . .

MANDY We're at the one across the street from Pennsylvania Station.

ANDY And Madison Square Garden too!

TAFFY It's the Statler-Hilton you're both at.

ANDY Sorry, Miss, but we're both feeling no pain . . .

MANDY We're on our honeymoon.

TAFFY Congratulations.

ANDY This is probably going to be the best time of our lives!

MANDY It's really going to be the most beautiful time of our lives.

TAFFY It's some life, isn't it?

ANDY It sure is!

MANDY It's just perfect.

TAFFY It sucks . . . !

ANDY What was that?!

MANDY I must be hearing things.

ANDY We're both really smashed!

TAFFY I didn't say a thing.

ANDY Are you angry at us, Miss?

TAFFY Taffy's the name.

MANDY Hi, Taffy.

ANDY How are you, Taffy?

TAFFY I'm rotten!

MANDY Oh? I'm sorry . . .

TAFFY I appreciate it. But don't be. We ask for what we get. And I'm getting a lot of flack these days. What is this thing called *love*, anyway?! It's supposed to be such a beautiful thing. If it's supposed to be such a beautiful thing thing: then why am I suffering the way I'm suffering, you, tell me that! I've got this lover, see? And I'm in love with . . . *this person,* see? I am so madly in love with *this* person that it really scares me almost all of the time simply because I think I might just simply be going half-mad half of the time simply because of this completely mad love affair that I'm so happily *madly* involved in . . . with *this* person. My lover is just simply great-looking and just so gorgeous well, you wouldn't believe it! My lover is great and gorgeous and loves to wear all of the Gucci things in life. Well, that costs money, lots of money. My lover doesn't work. This lovely luscious person whom I love so much just simply lounges aroud our little—but lovely—apartment, all day long and all night long, watching television, playing records, reading fashion magazines, bathing, showering, shampooing, bubble-bathing-it, napping, walking our pretty pet poodle whose name is Pat, meaning it could mean it'ts Patrick or Patricia or both—who knows?!—everything is so complicated these days! Or playing with our two cats whose names are Brick and Rock, by the way, and walking on that sweet promenade along the East River not too far from where the Mayor lives, and bouncing along over to the Public Library, the main branch: on Fifth Avenue, because she claims it's the perfect place and the perfect atmosphere to do her meditating and research and thinking because she claims she really needs to, simply because she says she's writing a book on what true love and real love between two people is actually all about!

MANDY (*Whispering*)   She said; she, Andy . . .

ANDY (*WHISPERING back*)   Shhhhhhh . . . !

TAFFY   What does she know?! I should be writing the book, not her!

MANDY (*Whispering*)   Did you hear her, Andy? She said it again . . .

ANDY (*Whispering back again*)   Honey, will you be quiet? You know how things like this turn me on . . . !

MANDY (*Still whispering*)   Oh, Andy . . . !

ANDY (*Whispering loudly*)   Will you be quiet so I can hear her?!

TAFFY   But I love her, and that's what really counts, and what more can I tell you? I love her more than anything else alive. . . . and it's very real and very romantic and even very religious too, in a very raunchy-rich way. Everytime I say to her: 'I *love* you, I *love* you, I *love* you!, I'm *in* love with you, I'm *in* love with you, I'm *in* love with you! I'm *so* in love with you, I'm *so* in love with you, I'm *so* in love with you!': Well, I mean it all, too, with all my heart and soul! Oh, God: I've said them all a million times to her already. And I don't mind it at all, either. I just simply wish that she would say something back to me once in awhile. Being in bed is just simply *not* enough . . . !

ANDY (*Still whispering*)   This is New York, Mandy. Sometimes I think that maybe we should move here.

MANDY (*Still whispering*)   Not me . . . never . . . !

TAFFY   Well, this is it. Here we are. I got you brand-new-honey-mooners all safe and sound back to your Statler-Hilton Hotel across the street from both Madison Square Garden and Pennsylvania Station.

MANDY (*Still whispering*)   Is she being sarcastic?

ANDY (*Still whispering*)   No, no. She's being friendly and funny.
(ANDY *pays the fare to* TAFFY *and then he gets out of the
taxicab with* MANDY)

TAFFY   You've got change coming, mister, lots of it . . .

ANDY   That's okay miss . . .

TAFFY   You're being too kind.

ANDY   That's because I like you a whole lot.

MANDY   Andy . . . ?

ANDY   Shut up!

TAFFY   I really believe you . . .

ANDY   I hope so . . .

MANDY   I'm sorry . . .

TAFFY   Forget it.

ANDY   I wish I could get it all out the way you just got it all out.

TAFFY   Let me tell you something: I don't believe it: I don't
believe that I let it all out the way I just let it all out. I've never
told anybody: especially my passengers. I always pretend. Or I
don't say a thing. (*There is a pause*) And so . . .

ANDY   You don't have to say anything . . .

TAFFY   But I . . .

ANDY   It was the best taxi ride I'll ever have . . .

MANDY   Me too . . . !

TAFFY   Thank you, both of you. I guess it all has to do with the
fact that you're both pretty goddam real deep down inside, no

matter what, you're both pretty goddam innocent, which also means that you're both pretty open, which also means that you're both pretty understanding and patient, which also means, finally, in the end, that you're both pretty much together, whether you think so or not, and you're not really square and country-folk and small-town hicks, but that you're both really just plain honest and human and there's no phoniness and no trying to put on airs and something that you're not, and, finally: well, there's just no bullshit with you kind of people! Pardon my language! But I just think the two of you are super and just plain terrific! And now: get out of here! Because I don't want to start crying in front of the two of you! I'm a walking, driving nervous breakdown and I'm just about ready to ball, and I don't mean the kind of balling that you both might think I mean either! Ciao! And goodbye! And good luck! And God bless; And I love you both! I had two straight Wild Turkey's before I came on duty; Can't you both tell?! And I don't want to start crying like a baby! Good luck! I hope your marriage lasts forever, I really do; I wish I was as happy and as innocent and as *real* as I want to believe that the two of you are! Goodbye, goodbye, goodbye! Before I start to cry! And thanks, so much, for the tremendous tip! I could really use it! *She's* an expensive love affair, to put it mildly!

ANDY   It was nice talking to you, Taffy . . .

TAFFY   Same here . . .

MANDY   Same here, too, Taffy . . .
(ANDY *and* MANDY *find it hard to leave* TAFFY, *but eventually they do*)

TAFFY (*To herself*)   How did I get into this? I can't stand it!
(*And then* TAFFY *goes to another telephone booth. She dials*)

TAFFY   Hello?! Hello?! Hello?! Now what's that all about?!
(*We hear a terrible nerve-wrecking sound coming over the public-address system: it is quite maddening*)

TAFFY   What's going on?!
(TAFFY *hangs up the telephone and then, frantically, she dials the same number again. But now she gets a busy*

signal: it is loud and sharp and nerve-shattering through the theatre)

TAFFY   I can't stand it!
(TAFFY *hangs up*)

TAFFY   Goddammitt! Oh . . . help . . . !
(TAFFY *is quite beside herself with frustration and anxious sadness all at the same time*)

(THE SECOND COUPLE *enters:* LADDIE *and* LORNA)

LORNA   She's adorable.

LADDIE   Who you talking about?

LORNA   That adorable taxicab driver over there.

LADDIE   Oh, yeah! A woman taxicab driver! What do you think, Lorna . . . ?

LORNA   About what?

LADDIE   About *her?*

LORNA   I told you: I think she's adorable.

LADDIE   What does that mean?

LORNA   You tell me, Laddie. You seem to be very hip and very aware of the whole scene: and what could really happen because of the whole adorable scene. I mean, darling: you're always so turned on by *Oui* Magazine and *Playboy* Magazine . . .

(TAFFY *has just lit up her "tenth" cigarette while she sits waiting at the steering-wheel of her idle taxicab, and while she turns on her portable radio. It begins to play: "All Because of You" by Barry White. She looks trance-like as she tries to listen to the music and the singing that's coming over her portable radio*)

LORNA   And all of those pornographic movies you've taken me to: all of those terribly heterosexual pornographic films made especially with the terribly heterosexual male in mind where they always have that token scene wherein two very lovely ladies are making love to each other, of, wherein, two very lovely ladies indulge in open sex and free love-making along with a terrible happy and terribly contented heterosexual male—just like you, Laddie,—wherein it's all quite stimulating and quite adorable for someone like the horny likes of you: my horny Laddie-Boy!

LADDIE   I'm gonna *come* right here, on First Avenue, with the soft splashing sounds of the East River going along with me . . . and *you* . . . if you don't stop talking the way you've been talking . . . even though I love every second of it!

TAFFY (*Suddenly*)   My cab's empty if you want it!

LADDIE   We want it!

TAFFY   Good! Then hop into it!

LORNA   She really *is* adorable, Laddie . . .

LADDIE   I know, I know . . . !

TAFFY   Where to?

LADDIE   The Village.

LORNA   Not my place, Laddie? My roommate's home for the weekend. Your place, Laddie.

LADDIE   Okay, okay. The corner of Park and Eighty-Sixth Street. (*To* TAFFY) You wanna come?

TAFFY   You talking to me?

LADDIE   I think so.

TAFFY   Come where?

LADDIE   To my place.

TAFFY   Your place?

LADDIE   Yes . . .

TAFFY   It doesn't seem right . . .

LADDIE   Why do you say that?

TAFFY   Well, you do have another woman with you, and . . .

LORNA   I don't mind!

TAFFY   Oh . . . ?

LADDIE   Okay, then . . . ?

LORNA   We're waiting for your answer: Ms. Adorable!

TAFFY   Well, my answer is that I'd probably get caught . . .

LORNA   Get caught?!

TAFFY   I mean I would get caught being off the job which means
that I would lose the job which I cannot afford to have happen
to me at the moment. You see, I've got this man back in our
apartment, this boy-friend of mine, and I love him very much!
Listen: I've never loved anybody the way I love him!
       (LADDIE *and* LORNA *are turned off and disappointed*)

LADDIE   But maybe you need a break from your ole' man.

LORNA   My Laddie's right.

TAFFY   I don't know. I don't think so. You see: my ole' man is a
very rare and precious person. I mean to say that I'd do anything for him just so's I knew it was a guarantee that I wouldn't
lose him.

LADDIE   Oh, really . . .

LORNA   I'm really disappointed . . .

TAFFY   My lover is a very beautiful man, a very gorgeous cat and I'm just simply not about to turn him off in any way. He's also a good person too.

LADDIE   Then why are you hacking a cab during the early hours of the morning?

LORNA   That's what I was thinking.

TAFFY   Because I told you before: I love him! I'm in love with this very special man like I've never been in love with any other man in my whole life! And there have been a lot of other men in my life before this one, but none of them could ever compare to the fantastic likes of him!

LADDIE   What's his name?

LORNA   Yes, by all means! Tell us the name of this modern Prince Charming!

TAFFY (*Quickly*)   Adam! That's it: Adam!

LADDIE   And your Eve!

LORNA   No, She's Teresa. It says so right there: Teresa A. O'Malley. On her license . . .

LADDIE   What's the A. stand for, Teresa?

LORNA   That's just what I was going to ask?

TAFFY   It's Ann . . .

LADDIE   Teresa Ann O'Malley.

TAFFY   But everybody has always called me by my nickname . . .

LORNA   Which is . . . ?

TAFFY   Taffy.

LADDIE   Taffy is nice and sweet . . .

LORNA To eat and have fun with . . .

LADDIE You can really do what you want with taffy candy.

TAFFY What does that mean?

LORNA It means you can control it . . .

LADDIE Shape it . . .

LORNA Manipulate it . . .

LADDIE Just like clay . . .

LORNA When I was a little girl I really did things with saltwater taffy in my mouth from Atlantic City . . .

LADDIE It was a sweet and a powerful trip!
    (*They both begin to giggle softly*)

TAFFY What's so funny?

LADDIE We want you to join us . . .

LORNA Tonight . . . !

TAFFY But I can't.

LADDIE She won't give in . . .

LORNA I can see . . .
    (LADDIE *embraces* LORNA *and they remain in a kissing clutch during the rest of* TAFFY's *speech*)

TAFFY My boy-friend—Adam—can't really find a job these days. He's an engineer, but a very gifted engineer, and it's so hard for people to see the genius in him. And so he just simply continues to study engineering, day and night, while he and I live together—as two very, *very* happy lovers!—and I don't mind bringing home the paycheck every week because I know that, no matter what, I would do anything for him, just simply because I know that he would do anything for me. It may all sound corny and cliche-ridden and just too sugary and too

romantic in this day and age that we all live in: but I would die
for him! And I think that he would also die for me! We both
have such a great thing going: I can't imagine life being any
other way for me—and him—than the way it is right now. I
love it!

(LADDIE *and* LORNA *come out of their "clutch"*)

LADDIE   This   is   it . . . We're   here.   One   last   time,
Taffy . . . ?

TAFFY   I can't.

LORNA   One last time, Taffy . . . ?

TAFFY   I really can't!
(LADDIE *hands* TAFFY *the taxi-fare. She immediately gives
him his change back. He hands her a tip*)

TAFFY   Thank you very much. Good night.

LADDIE   Good night.

LORNA   I hope that you're night is going to be as good as ours is.

LADDIE   You had your chance.

LORNA   One more time?!

TAFFY (*Trying to smile*)   Good night.
(LADDIE *and* LORNA *exit*)

(TAFFY *jumps out of her taxicab and goes to another telephone booth. She dials. We hear the loud busy signal.*
TAFFY *is beside herself with nervousness*)

TAFFY   I can't stand it! I can't stand it! I can't stand it!
(JOANNA *enters. She jumps into* TAFFY'S *taxi immediately*)

JOANNA   Please take me home!

TAFFY (*Walking slowly back to her taxi*)   Where do you live?

JOANNA   I'm at The Barbizon at the moment, and I hate it, But
that's life.

TAFFY   I forgot where it's at.

JOANNA   I'll direct you. Just follow my instructions. Lexington and the early sixties somewhere. When I see it I'll tell you.

TAFFY   It's a hotel for women, isn't it?

JOANNA   That's right. And that's why I hate it. Actually, I should really love it because I'm really into women. I've always been into women and never really know it until I came to New York from St. Louis in order to study high-fashion modeling. I love women! A whole lot! I went to this gay place tonight. It was really a party in an apartment: All women: some of them so beautiful. But everyone of them were playing such self-indulgent games, etcetra, if you know what I mean? By the way, are you gay?

TAFFY   What?

JOANNA   I asked you if you were gay. A Lesbian? I am!

TAFFY   I don't think I am . . .

JOANNA   You mean you don't know?

TAFFY   No, I do know! I'm not gay! I'm not a Lesbian! I am very proud to say that I'm madly in love with this very handsome and beautiful man whose at home right now writing his novel which he has been working on for eight months while I hack this taxicab in order to keep us both from starving to death!

JOANNA   I find it hard to believe you.

TAFFY   He's very special.

JOANNA   Oh, really?

TAFFY   He's the sort of man who comes around once in a lifetime.

JOANNA   I see.

TAFFY   I feel so lucky.

JOANNA   I'm glad for you.

TAFFY   I love it when he doesn't shave for two days.

JOANNA   How come?

TAFFY   Because it's so nice and rough on my skin and it tickles and it . . .

JOANNA   You know something?

TAFFY   What?

JOANNA   I find it very to believe you.
          (TAFFY *stiffens*)

TAFFY   You do?

JOANNA   Yes, I do.

TAFFY   Why do you?

JOANNA   Because you're just too nervous and too desperate and you give off such anxious vibes.

TAFFY   Anxious vibes?

JOANNA   The vibrations you give off are hung-up ones.

TAFFY   Hung-up ones?

JOANNA   You know what I mean. I mean, if you don't care my telling you this, and you can tell me to fuck-off if you want to, but I think this man you're talking about is really a woman, and this woman is really shitting all over you, and you're taking it all, because you love this woman very much, more than she loves you . . .

TAFFY   Stop it!
          (TAFFY *stops the taxicab very suddenly: without any warning*)

JOANNA   Why are we stopping like this?

TAFFY   Because I have to make an emergency telephone call,
that's why! You're going to have to wait for me until I come
back!
(JOANNA *half-smiles*)

JOANNA   It's all right with me.
(TAFFY *leaves the taxicab. She goes to a corner telephone
booth and dials. She is instantly relieved: there is no busy
signal this time. She lets the telephone ring for about four
rings: and then there is an answer*)

TAFFY (*Into the mouthpiece nervously*)   Oh . . . it's you,
honey! . . . Well, I'm sorry, but . . . But the line was busy
for so long! . . . I'm not shouting! . . . I thought that
maybe you had it off the hook . . . Please . . . ?! . . .
No, don't say that to me, no! . . . What . . . ?! . . . But
I just wanted to call again that's all, I just wanted to hear your
voice again, that's all! . . . But I was thinking, well, I was
thinking: that I just don't feel too good all of a sudden, and so, I
thought that I would quit earlier than usual and come back
home . . . okay? . . . It's not . . . okay? . . . But I
have this devastating headache, honey, and I really need to
come home and take care of myself . . . and to be with
you . . . ! No, no: don't hang up!
(*It is obvious that there is a hang-up.* TAFFY *is now a
combination of pure sadness and pure frustration; she is
trembling; she tries to fight the tears of rage and unhappi-
ness. Eventually, she goes back to her taxicab.* JOANNA *is
still waiting*)

JOANNA (*After a pause*)   Look, I'm very forward. I think I'm
very together. I'll be perfectly frank with you. I like you. You
turn me on. Let's go somewhere together. I think it'll do us
both a whole lot of good.
(TAFFY *is driving the taxicab fast now; she does not respond to* JOANNA *at* first)

TAFFY (*Finally*)   I have two jobs. I have this one and I have
another one during the daytime. I work as a secretary at CBS.
It's hard for me. I only sleep four hours a day. The other four
are spent awake with *her!* God knows what she does during the
times that I hack this cab and type letters and answer tele-
phones. But I suppose I don't care because she makes me

happier than anybody else I've ever known. And I do dream a lot. I dream that eventually she'll see the light and then everything will turn out okay: the way I'm always dreaming it will turn out okay. She can be mean and miserable and sadistic, and I take it all, simply because, well: how can you explain one's feelings, one's passions, or whatever-you-want-to-call-them?! My philosophy is to go along with it all. I believe that one's heart controls everything. And that's all I have to say to you. What's your name?

JOANNA   Joanna.

TAFFY   Well, here we are. Your destination.
(JOANNA *writes something on a small piece of paper. She hands it to* TAFFY)

JOANNA   Here.

TAFFY   What is it?

JOANNA   If you ever feel like calling.

TAFFY   Thanks . . .
(JOANNA *pays* TAFFY *the fare;* TAFFY *returns the change;* JOANNA *returns a tip; then she climbs out of the taxicab and goes running off*)

TAFFY   Thanks . . . again . . .
(TAFFY *gets out of the taxicab. She goes to what seems like a jukebox in some bar. She makes a selection. It is Barry White again: singing: "All Because Of You." Then she goes to another telephone booth. She dials. The line is still busy. The sound of it seems louder than ever as the music continues to play. Now the busy signal is almost deafening throughtout the theatre: it drowns out the music.* TAFFY *stands there, holding the receiver in her hand. At first she begins to laugh, somewhat hysterically; then; suddenly: she is weeping softly*)

Curtain

Tripper's Taxi

THE PEOPLE OF THE PLAY
(*as they speak*)

TRIPPER: a ''stoned-looking'' man who is really handsome with longish sandy-colored hair and a firm trim physique; and it is somewhat difficult to imagine him not ''stoned-looking'': there is something pleasantly incorrigible about it, even strangely sexual; he wears a white T-shirt with bright red letters on it: it says: *You're Gonna Get It!;* he is probably in his late 20's and he is like a restless cat, a ''stoned'' one, that is.

LOVELY: her name fits her almost perfectly and she is about 25 years old.

MOMMY: a good looking woman who is possibly close to 50 but looks younger.

DADDY: a good-looking man who also looks young for his age, but who is also close to 50.

WHERE THEY ARE

In a taxicab on its way to The World Trade Center.

WHEN

Suppertime during the present time.

Tripper's Taxi

When the curtain goes up we see an empty taxicab. We also see the "dangling display" all along the inside of the whole expanse of the front window of the taxicab: a souvenir "big apple," a tiny toy teddy-bear, a Christmas peppermint candy cane, a valentine heart, a Kennedy half-dollar, a silver star, and a gold crucifix. Eventually, TRIPPER *enters. He carries a small rabbit's foot with him; he hangs it into the "dangling display" of his taxicab, and then he makes a sweeping gesture with his right hand all across the inside front window so that everything that is hanging is now in dangling motion. He laughs to himself, and then he sits down behind the wheel, half-mesmerized by the swaying array of movement before him: a strange-happy smile on his face.*

TRIPPER (*Out loud, to himself*)   Gee whiz! Weeeeeee! What a nice sight to see! A real trip! A real journey! A real adventure! What a wonderful vacation! (*A pause*) A souvenir "big apple," a tiny toy teddy-bear, a Kennedy half-dollar, a silver star, a Christmas peppermint candy cane, a valentine heart, a gold crucifix, and now: a lucky rabbit's foot. I've got it made: I've got everything I want: I'm the happiest guy in the world!
　　(LOVELY, MOMMY, *and* DADDY *enter*)

LOVELY   Oh, look: Mommy and Daddy: we have a taxicab waiting for us! Taxi . . . !

MOMMY   We've always been so lucky about things like this . . . !

DADDY   We've always been lucky about everything in general . . . !

TRIPPER   Hop in, ladies! Hop in, mister!
　　(LOVELY, MOMMY, *and* DADDY *all climb into the back seat*)

TRIPPER (*Starting up the motor*)   Where to?

DADDY   The World Trade Center.

LOVELY   We're going to have dinner way up in the sky. . . .

MOMMY   In The-Windows-On-The-World . . . !

TRIPPER (*Driving off*)   The World Trade Center it is!

LOVELY   Are you in show business, cabbie?

TRIPPER   The-Windows-On-The-World it is!

MOMMY   I'll bet he's an actor, Lovely.

TRIPPER   We're on our way!

DADDY   He looks like he's not with us to me. Do you both know what I mean? Lovely? Mommy? He looks like he's in another world to me. Maybe we should get out and find ourselves another cab. What do you think?

LOVELY   No . . .

MOMMY   I think this is fine . . .

LOVELY   I like him . . .

TRIPPER (*To himself*)   Quay . . . loods!

DADDY   He's not right for you, Lovely. First of all: he's hacking a cab . . .

TRIPPER (*To himself, smiling*)   Quaaaaaaaa . . . loooooods!

DADDY   Which is not for you, Lovely. And second of all: he's a drunk or a drug addict or a metal patient . . .

LOVELY   Oh, Daddy: you just don't want to give me up, that's all.

MOMMY   Lovely's right, Daddy. You want her to stay with us forever, isn't that right, Daddy?

DADDY   No, that's not right. I've always wanted Lovely—*our* Lovely—to find a good man for herself . . .

MOMMY   Other than you, right, Daddy . . . ?

LOVELY   Isn't that right, Daddy?

DADDY   Yes, that's right.

MOMMY   Well, I think our cabbie is just adorable for our Lovely, don't you think so, Lovely?

LOVELY   Well, yes, now: come to think of it: I do.

DADDY   I don't!

MOMMY   Are you jealous, Daddy?

DADDY   No!

LOVELY   Well, do you feel threatened then, Daddy?

DADDY   Of course not!

LOVELY   What's your name, driver?
(TRIPPER *doesn't answer*)

MOMMY I don't think he heard you? Driver: what's your name?
(TRIPPER *still does not answer*)

DADDY   Driver?! My daughter asked you a question: and you didn't answer her! And then my wife asked you a question as well: and you didn't answer her, either! They both asked you what your name is! Be a gentleman! Answer them!

TRIPPER   (*Finally*) I'm Tripper . . . not because I trip over things . . . I'm very graceful, in fact . . . I'm called Tripper because I am always taking a trip, I'm always on a trip, preparing for a trip, or getting over a trip, or thinking about the trips that I haven't taken yet, or . . .

DADDY   Listen to him!

MOMMY   Shhhhhhh . . . !

DADDY   He's exactly what I thought he was from the beginning!

TRIPPER   I'm just plain ole' Tripper who happens to be the happiest guy in the world!

LOVELY   He's becoming very appealing to me, everybody!

DADDY   I know what you're getting at, Lovely.

DADDY   I'm not the least bit interested in what the two of you are saying. I'm only interested in my relationship to the two of you in relation to me. I'm the husband and I'm the father, and you're the mother, and you're the daughter, and I want us to be together forever. We don't need anybody else: the three of us . . . just like the three bears, in a way . . . and we certainly don't need a cab-driver in our lives . . . not my wife, not my daughter, and certainly not me! (*Suddenly*) *Cabbie!*

TRIPPER   Yeah . . . man . . . ?

DADDY   Drive faster! Do you understand me?!

TRIPPER   Sure thing . . . man.

DADDY   I am a family man. I love my family. Sometimes, well, sometimes, when the three of us have been drinking too much champagne, well, the three of us all sleep in the same bed together. It's all very innocent, of course . . .

MOMMY (*Giggling*)   Oh, Daddy . . . !

LOVELY (*Giggling too*)   Tsk, tsk, Daddy . . . !

DADDY   But it's true, ladies, and like I said before: it's all very innocent too.

MOMMY   What would we ever do without you, Daddy?

DADDY   I think you'd both have a hard time.

LOVELY   We could never, ever do without you, Daddy.

DADDY   Now that's the sort of talk that I like to hear. We're going to have a wonderful time on top of The World Trade Center, dining and wining in The-Windows-On-The-World, spending as much money as we want, simply because we have all of the money that anybody could ever want. (*A pause*) Someday, well, someday, Lovely: my lovely daughter, someday you'll find the right man. Take my word for it. I know that the three of us have been drinking a lot today, and so, maybe that's why our cabbie, Tripper up there, looks good to the two of you . . . in a way he even looks good to me . . . but that's because he's not like us, that's all . . . just the way that we're not like him at all, either. (*A pause*) We can't just settle for anybody, or anything right now. That would be a shame, and a waste. We've got to go on looking, searching, until we find the right person, The perfect human being. (*A pause*) That's going to take more time than we thought. But, in the end, it will have been worth it, believe me.

>   (*A pause, as both* LOVELY *and* MOMMY *look at* DADDY *with proud, loving eyes*)

TRIPPER (*Finally*)   I've been listening to everything that's going on back there. Yeah, man! Yeah, everybody! We gotta go on looking! We gotta go on searching! I can buy all of that! I mean: I'm the happiest man in the world . . . but it doesn't mean that it's the end for me. No way! It's the beginning: ya' all understand me?! I take everything, and I've tried everything. I'm still taking, and I'm still trying. And do you all wanna know why?! Because I wanna be even happier than the happiest guy in the world, that's why!

>   (*But* LOVELY, MOMMY, *and* DADDY *aren't even listening to* TRIPPER *now. Instead, they are all gazing at one another like moonstruck lovers: it is almost embarrassing to watch*)

TRIPPER (*A pause*)   They weren't even listening to me . . .

>   (TRIPPER *looks like he might even burst into tears for a split second*)

TRIPPER (*Pulling up*)   Here we are . . . The world Trade Center . . .

DADDY (*Coming out of his "trance"*)   That was fast . . .

MOMMY (*Coming out of her "trance"*) He's a good cab-driver . . .

LOVELY (*Coming out of her "trance"*) I'll bet he's even better than we think he is . . .

DADDY   Never mind now, Lovely.

MOMMY   Daddy's right, Lovely . . .

LOVELY   Okay, okay . . . I understand.
(LOVELY, DADDY, *and* MOMMY *climb out of the taxicab*)

MOMMY   Keep the change, Tripper.
(DADDY *hands* TRIPPER *the money*)

MOMMY   Good luck, Tripper . . .

LOVELY   Goodbye, Tripper . . . !

TRIPPER   Oh, yes! Thanks for the tip! And good luck . . . and good-bye too.
(LOVELY, MOMMY, *and* DADDY *all exit together*)

TRIPPER (*After a moment*) I'm the happiest guy in the world, man! If only everybody could be a sixteenth as happy as me! But I deserve it, because I worked on it, I worked for it, I never stopped working at it. Everytime I got depressed, I tried everything. And I bought all kinds of things too. And all of the girls I know: they'll always love me. And my friends and relatives too: they'll always love me too. It would be pretty dumb not to be able to love the happiest person you ever met in your life . . .
(TRIPPER *takes in a big breath, and then he sighs, loud and long. He reaches for the heart-shaped valentine box that hangs along the dashboard. He removes the lid rather secretlike and takes out a handful of pills. He swallows them all down with coffee from his thermos jug. He smiles wildly, and then, silently, he climbs out of his taxicab. He stands and stretches. He looks up at the sky. His smile remains*)

TRIPPER   The World Trade Center . . . two buildings . . . I've got a choice . . . I'll create my own "windows-on-the-world'' . . . I'll zoom to the top in some elevator . . . and then I'll float down, afterwards . . . first in some fast crowded elevator . . . and then, afterwards: all by myself, not fast, either, but slow, and definite, and absolute, and floating: downward, landing on top of the world on my own two feet, walking away then, heading for the next planet . . . without Daddy and Mommy and Lovely, who will still be trying to make up their minds . . . (*A pause*) You just wait and see, *you just wait and see, YOU JUST WAIT AND SEE . . . !*

(TRIPPER *walks away from his taxicab; it is as though he is floating*)

Blackout

Toddy's Taxi

THE PEOPLE OF THE PLAY
(*as they speak*)

TODDY: a truly terrific-looking man who is just about 30 years old, even though there is something extremely "teen-aged" about him; he is bold and brash and full of balls, and very nicely "up-front" about things, and he presents a very beautiful—sort of strangely "spiritual"—first impression; he dresses in faded blue jeans that are a perfect fit for his hard slim physique; he also wears an immaculate white dress shirt with a bright red necktie made in India: he also wears a pair of expensive beige-looking leather boots and a matching cap on his head which he "nervously" takes on-and-off a whole lot; and instead of smoking he chews gum every so often.

GIGI: a pretty-looking woman in her middle 20's

MIMI: another pretty-looking woman who is also in her mid-20's

SPEED: a good-looking man who is probably in his early 30's.

WHERE THEY ARE

In a taxicab on its way to Kennedy Airport.

WHEN

Early nighttime during the 1970's.

(NOTE: As in TAFFY'S TAXI: GIGI, MIMI, and SPEED can be played by the same actors and actresses once again; and the setting's overall design should be in the same related keeping; and TODDY'S TAXI should follow TAFFY'S TAXI.)

41

Toddy's Taxi

*When the curtain goes up there is little noise to be heard,
except for various sounds of muffled New York traffic in the quiet
background. The lighting is bright and midnight blue even if it's
early evening, and the moon is big and beaming and round and
full, and the night is extra-clear: with lots of twinkling stars that
are very clear up there in the dark smooth-looking sky. Eventually,* TODDY *appears. He is unwrapping a pack of chewing gum
which he has just bought. He places the gum in his mouth, and
then he walks to his waiting taxicab. He sits down in the driver's
seat. He looks in the mirror: doing a real thorough job of posing
and examining himself. He takes off his cap, fixes his hair a little
bit. Then he puts the cap back on. Then he turns on the radio. We
hear the opening strains of Stravinsky's* The Firebird! *We can tell
that* TODDY *is pleased by this. Then he takes out a small pocket
mirror. He begins to look at himself from side views, etcetera, in
both his pocket mirror and the mirror of the taxicab; he takes off
his cap: he is looking at himself from profile angles via both the
mirrors. He is finished now. We hear a voice belonging to a man.
It calls out: "Taxi! Taxi!" But* TODDY *ignores it. He puts away
his pocket mirror. He starts up the taxicab and pulls away as we
still hear the man's voice: "Taxi! Taxi!"* TODDY *puts his cap back
on. He chews his gum. Suddenly blows a bubble with it. He
begins to laugh because he is surprised that he has bubble-gum
instead of chewing gum. We hear another male voice: "Hey, taxi!
Taxi!" But* TODDY *ignores it all. He listens to "The Firebird"
instead, and he blows an occasional bubble with his bubble-gum
instead. Finally, we hear a female voice: "Taxi! Taxi!"* TODDY *is
very attentive all of a sudden. "Taxi!" He pulls his cap straight
down over his forehead. He checks himself out in the front mirror.
Now we hear another voice of a different female: "Taxi!"* TODDY
*pulls up his cab and stops, then takes his bubble-gum from out of
his mouth and gets rid of it in the ashtray of the taxicab. He gives
himself a very good look in the mirror this time: he wets his lips,
and runs his wet tongue across his teeth. By this time:* GIGI *and*
MIMI *have appeared, along with* SPEED *who is really drunk. The
two women are giving him as much support as possible)*

43

TODDY   Oh, wait a minute now . . . !
    (TODDY *is not too pleased*)

GIGI   What's the matter?!

TODDY   Everthing's the matter!

MIMI   Just what *is* the matter?!

TODDY   Everything!

GIGI   What, for instance?!

TODDY   I'm not in the mood!

MIMI   You're not in the mood for what?!

SPEED (*Drunkenly*) He's not in the mood . . . for anybody
. . . whose been drinking too fuckin' much . . . that's what
he's not in the mood for . . . !

GIGI (*To* SPEED)   Shhhhhh!

MIMI (*To* SPEED)   Be quiet, please?!

SPEED   Shit . . . !

GIGI   We've got to get him on a plane, fast!

MIMI   Kennedy Airport, okay, driver?!

TODDY (*To* MIMI)   You're a real lady, I can tell.

MIMI   I am?

TODDY   Yep.

GIGI   What about me?

TODDY   You are too.

SPEED   Get me on that plane, goddammitt . . . !

(*Stravinsky's "The Firebird" continues to play in the background from the cab radio*)

TODDY   No way.

SPEED   Did I hear right . . . ?!

TODDY   Yep!

GIGI   Please, sir: don't pay any attention to him . . .

MIMI   He's been drinking a little too much which means that he's not responsible for his behavior at the moment, okay?

GIGI   Okay, sir?
        (TODDY *doesn't say a word at this point. Instead: he gats out of the taxicab. He stretches his body. It is as though he is showing off for the two women. Then he pretends to be bored by yawning luxuriously. The two women don't quite know what to do. And so: they begin to hand* SPEED'S *luggage to* TODDY)

TODDY   What's this all about?

GIGI   It's luggage . . .

MIMI   It's our friend's luggage . . .

SPEED   It's Gucci . . . so be careful . . . you understand, cabbie?!

TODDY   No way!
        (SPEED *falls to the sidewalk*)

GIGI   Oh, dear . . . !

MIMI   He's fallen . . . !

TODDY   He sure has.

SPEED (*Mumbling*)   Fuck . . . shit . . . goddammitt . . . !
        (GIGI *and* MIMI *make attempts at getting* SPEED *up from the sidewalk, but they don't have much luck at it*)

GIGI   Please, sir . . .

MIMI   Help us . . . !
(TODDY *stands with his hands on his hips. He takes off his cap and stuffs it carefully in his back pocket jeans*)

GIGI (*To* TODDY)   What are you doing?!

MIMI (*To* TODDY)   We need help!
(SPEED *is lying on his back now, on the sidewalk: half-mumbling to himself, drunkenly*)

GIGI (*To* TODDY)   We need your help!

MIMI (*To* TODDY)   Can't you see?!

TODDY   He's too drunk for me. That I can see.

GIGI   Please . . . ?

MIMI   Don't be so difficult . . .

TODDY   I never pick up drunks.

GIGI   Don't be so prudish . . .
(GIGI *and* MIMI *continue to try and get* SPEED *up on his feet again*)

TODDY   Prudish? Difficult? You two ladies just gotta be kidding, that's all there is to it. First of all: I'm the least difficult person in the world. Ask my friends. My relatives will tell you. Ask my wife! I don't have any kids, otherwise you could ask them too. As for being prudish? Well, you're both all wrong. Do you know what "Harder" is? It's a magazine that I subscribe to, see? It's even better than "Hustler" could ever think of being. And then there's "Deeper." Did you two ever hear of "Deeper"? Well, it's the best one of them all, and I subscribe to "Deeper" too. "Harder" and "Deeper." I get them both in the mail everytime they both come out, you see? So don't be saying that I'm prudish, okay?

SPEED (*Mumbling, struggling to get up*)   "Harder"? "Deeper"? What the fuck, what the fuck, what the hell is goin' on? Are we

all goin' to get laid in some kind of street gang-bang tonight?
Shit! That's not a bad idea . . . before I fly back to the wife
and the kids back in Seattle . . . well, it's all right by
me . . . I'd like something like that . . . for a nightcap
. . . before I get on that goddam plane, because, shit, I really
hate to fly anyway, and a nice nightcap in the form of a street
gang-bang tonight would be a very good way to take my fucking mind off of getting into that . . . frightening airplane
that's out there waiting for me . . . !

GIGI (*To* TODDY)   Please change your mind, sir?

MIMI (*To* TODDY)   Please . . . ?

TODDY   I have a confession to make.

GIGI   We don't have much time left!

MIMI   We really don't sir?

TODDY   Call me Toddy. You know: like a "hot toddy"? The
drink? That's me: Toddy. Sometimes people actually refer to
me as "Hot Toddy" instead of just plain ole' Toddy. I like it
too. Because, well, in case you've both never had a hot toddy
drink before, well, it's a very warm and very cozy drink to
have, let me tell you. Especially on cold windy nights when the
snow is really falling outside and you're glad to be inside
. . . with your "Hot Toddy." Do you know what I mean,
ladies?

GIGI   Oh, yes!

MIMI   We know what you mean!

TODDY   Ya' both sure?

GIGI   Oh, sure.

MIMI   For certain!

SPEED   Well . . . ?! What about it?!

TODDY   What about what, man?!

GIGI   Don't pay any attention to him Toddy . . .

MIMI   Yes, Toddy: he's really drunk, you know, and . . .

TODDY   I know!

SPEED   I'm not that . . . drunk! Honest . . . !

GIGI   Please, Speed!

MIMI   You can't miss that plane, no way!

SPEED   I know that I'm not that drunk. I can hear music . . .

TODDY   It's my radio, buddy.

SPEED   You can call me Speed . . . that's my name . . .
    Speed!

TODDY   It's my radio you're hearing, Speed.

SPEED   You gotta tasteful radio then, and you got taste too: just
    like your radio. What's your name again . . .?

TODDY   Toddy.

SPEED   Well, Toddy: you're a class-act taxicab driver . . .
    that's all I can say . . .

TODDY   Thanks.

GIGI   You're going to help us now, aren't you, Toddy?

MIMI   Aren't you?
    (*There is a pause. We hear the music in the background*)

TODDY   Okay.

GIGI   Thank you so much.

MIMI   You're very kind.

GIGI   Could you help us get Speed up off the ground and into
    your cab, please?

MIMI   Yes, he's heavier than he looks.
(TODDY *helps get* SPEED *to his feet, along with the assist-
ance of* GIGI *and* MIMI. *They all manage to get* SPEED *into
the back seat of the taxicab. And then* GIGI *and* MIMI *get in
also, sitting on each side of* SPEED. *In the meantime;*
TODDY *takes* SPEED's *luggage and shoves it in the backseat
with the three of them*)

TODDY   We're all set.
(TODDY *slams the door shut. Then he goes around to the
front door and climbs in also*)

SPEED   Why . . . are we so crowded back here . . . ?!

GIGI   Toddy: what about the trunk?

TODDY   What about the trunk?

MIMI   Well, couldn't you put Speed's luggage in the back trunk
of your taxicab?

TODDY   No!

SPEED   Listen to that music, will you . . . !

TODDY   Everybody ready?

SPEED   Stravinsky . . . "The Firebird Suite" . . . right on,
so they say these days . . . shit . . . !
(SPEED *passes out*)

GIGI   Oh, dear!

TODDY   What's the matter?

MIMI   He's passed out!

TODDY   Good!
(TODDY *starts up the taxicab, and then, off they all go*)

GIGI   Why do you say that?

MIMI   After all, he was a pleasant drunk.

TODDY   I didn't say he wasn't. It's just that now we'll have a little less noise, understand? Besides, he'll be able to sleep some of it off. (*A pause*) Also, it gives me a good chance to strike up a conversation with the two of you. What's your names?

GIGI   I'm Gigi.

TODDY   Hello, Gigi.

MIMI   And I'm Mimi.

TODDY   Hello, Mimi.
(TODDY *smiles back at both of them*)

GIGI   You have a lovely smile, Toddy . . .

MIMI   Such perfect-looking teeth.

TODDY   I've always taken care of them.

GIGI   You should do commercials for tooth paste.

MIMI   I can just see you on the back of some magazine.

TODDY   How do I break into something like that?

GIGI   Go to an agent.

MIMI   That's right.

TODDY   I'm sort of shy about things like that.

GIGI   You certainly don't seem shy.

MIMI   Gigi's right.

TODDY   But I really am.

GIGI   Well, you subscribe to those magazines for men that you were telling us about before . . .

MIMI   Yes. What were they called?

TODDY   "Harder" and "Deeper."

GIGI   That's not being shy.

MIMI   Especially since you also subcribe to them.

TODDY   I guess you're both right. (*A pause*) What do you two ladies do?

GIGI   Well, we're not shy at all.

MIMI   We're a team.

TODDY   Gigi and Mimi sounds like a team. What kind of team?

GIGI   Shall we tell him?

MIMI   I don't see why not. I mean what the hell.

GIGI   We're very, *very* expensive "ladies of the night" . . .

MIMI   Very, *very* expensive.

TODDY   Oh!

GIGI   Does that turn you on, Toddy?

TODDY   What?!

MIMI   What we've just told you about ourselves?

TODDY   (*A pause*) Yeah. Yeah . . . I guess it does. Sure. Sure . . . of course it does. (*A pause*) Do you always work in pairs? I mean: are you both always a team?

GIGI   Always!

MIMI   It's part of the deal.

TODDY   What's the deal?

GIGI   It's simple. Gigi and Mimi together. For whatever rich young out-of-town gentleman desires us . . .

TODDY   Oh?!

MIMI   Together. Along with the willing gentleman, who is also willing to pay a small fortune . . .

TODDY   Oh?!

GIGI   In order to be with us . . .

MIMI   Two willing ladies and one willing man having a grand ole' sexual time of it all!

TODDY   I see. (*A pause*) Do you mind if I ask you both something?

GIGI   Go ahead.

MIMI (*Laughing*)   As long as it's not too personal . . .

GIGI (*Also laughing*)   nor embarrassing . . . !

MIMI (*Still laughing*)   We're very shy and very secret, you know?

GIGI (*Still laughing*)   Don't tell our parents, Toddy.

MIMI (*Still laughing*)   God forbid if you did.

TODDY (*Trying to laugh with them*)   I promise I won't.

GIGI   So . . . ?

MIMI   What were you going to ask us?

TODDY (*A pause*)   Well . . . do you ever do it with a woman instead of a man? I mean is there ever three women involved instead?

GIGI   I knew you were going to ask that.

MIMI   Does that idea turn you on, Toddy?

TODDY (*A pause*)   Yes. A little bit, anyway.

GIGI   Well, sorry to disappoint you . . .

MIMI   But we never ever do it with the third person being a woman.

TODDY (*A pause*)   I was just wondering, that's all.
    (GIGI *and* MIMI *both light up cigarettes together*)

GIGI   Look at Speed's face, will you?

MIMI   He looks adorable, doesn't he?

GIGI   I hate to see him go back.

MIMI   So do I.

GIGI   But he said he'd be back in two weeks again.

MIMI   He also said that from now on he'd be coming in more often.

GIGI   I didn't know that.

MIMI   At least once a month, he told me.

GIGI   Terrific!

MIMI   That's what I say!
    (*A pause*)

GIGI   Toddy?

TODDY (*Who has been listening to everything*)   Yes?

GIGI   Do you always play classical music like that on your radio?

TODDY   Always.

MIMI   Most cabbies never play music like that.

TODDY   I play it because it makes me feel relaxed and restful. It also makes me feel less nervous and less uptight about my life. It's smooth and soothing and it makes me feel better than usual because I know that I can appreciate things like this: classical music. It's good for the soul, I guess. It keeps me in touch with the finer things in life, and I suppose, in a way, it makes me feel closer to God and to the finer spiritual things in life. It keeps me from being depressed, from being disturbed, from being despondent, from being desperate. When I listen to music like this sort of music, well, I'm able to keep myself in control. If I ever lost control I think that I would be a violent type of person. This way, I'm not violent at all. I'm a very peaceful human being because of the music that I always listen to. (*A pause*) I would probably have a nervous breakdown, or I'd go out of my mind, if it weren't for this kind of music that I love to listen to. (*A pause*) Remember before? I started to tell the two of you something? I started to say that I had something to confess? Well, it was really a stupid thing. (*A pause*)

GIGI   Well, tell us anyway.

MIMI   Yes, please do.

TODDY   I was going to tell you both that I never pick up men.

GIGI   What does that mean?

MIMI   I hope you don't pick up men.

TODDY   Oh no! I didn't mean it that way! I love women! I love women a whole lot!

GIGI   Thank God!

MIMI   I knew you did!

TODDY   My God: I wouldn't know what to do without women. I would probably become a vegetable if it weren't for the beautiful women that walk the face of this earth. God, I really worship them all! You have no idea! Anyway, what I started to say before was that I never pick up men, I never stop for a male passenger. I never indulge with a fare if it's a man who tries to hail down my taxicab. Right before I heard the two of you hail me down I passed up two different male voices. Who wants to have a man's fare? I'd rather lose a few extra bucks a night. Sometimes, if there are too many men on the streets in search of a cab, well, I just flash on my "off-duty" sign. Let me tell you both something: it's a good thing you're both women. Otherwise Speed, your drunken friend here, wouldn't be in this cab with the rest of us, and that's the honest-to-God truth.

GIGI (*A pause*)   Well, we should feel very lucky.

MIMI   Yes.

TODDY   I should feel very lucky too. Because of the two of you.

GIGI   Well, Toddy: thank you.

MIMI   And now, since you love women so much, how about doing us another favor, okay?

TODDY   What's that?

MIMI   How about stopping for a minute or two?

TODDY   Why?

MIMI   Because it's really awfully cramped and crowded back here.

GIGI   Yes, Mimi's right. Could you please put Speed's luggage in the back trunk?

MIMI   We'll help you.

TODDY   No!

GIGI   You're going to get an even bigger tip than we had planned on before, if you do.

TODDY   I'm really not interested in a bigger tip. (*A pause*) I know! (*Laughing*) How about Speed?!

GIGI   Speed?!

TODDY   Your rich gentleman-friend from Seattle: Speed!

MIMI   How about him for what?!

TODDY   How about putting Speed in the back trunk?!

GIGI   Very funny, Toddy.

MIMI   *Not* funny at all, Toddy. We both love Speed.

TODDY   Bad joke, huh, ladies-of-the-night?

GIGI   Right on.

MIMI   What's the big deal about the back trunk anyway?

TODDY   (*A pause*)   If I tell you both, will you promise not to tell anybody else?

GIGI   I promise.

MIMI   So do I.

TODDY   Well, you see, I'm married, first of all. No children, but I'm still married. I wouldn't want my wife to know. (*A pause*) I've got a woman in the back trunk. (*A pause*) So now you both understand why I want it to be kept a secret. My wife would be heart-broken if she ever found out. (*A pause*) Promise you won't tell?

GIGI   So you've got a woman in the back trunk, huh?

TODDY   Shhhhhh! Someone might hear you!

MIMI   Tsk, tsk. Toddy . . . ?

TODDY   Yes, Mimi?

MIMI   Another bad joke, right, Toddy?
(TODDY *laughs, turning around to face the two of them; and while* SPEED *is softly snoring now*)

GIGI   Yeah, Toddy.

MIMI   But you're still terribly disarming.

TODDY   (*A pause*)   Thanks for the compliment. I need to hear a nice surprise compliment once in awhile. We all do. And I apologize for the latest bad joke.

GIGI (*A pause*)   What's your wife like?

MIMI   I was also going to ask that.

TODDY   You might not believe it, but I'll tell you anyway. I met her on the subway a couple of years ago. I was sitting in a subway car, all by myself, reading the latest copy of Penthouse—by the way, I hardly ever buy Penthouse anymore, only "Harder" and "Deeper" now, what great magazines they are!—anyway, I was riding the subway one afternoon, when all of a sudden this beautiful-looking young thing—she was nineteen, which, of course, I found out later on—this beautiful, gorgeous young creature began to pass out little folded-type cards and they were all different colors. When she came to me she half-smiled at me, and then I half-smiled back at her, and then she handed me a light blue, folding card, and I liked that right away because light blue, is one of my favorite colors. The card said: "Hello! I am a deaf person, I am also a mute person. I am selling this *deaf-mute education system* card to make my living. Will you kindly buy one? Pay any price that you wish! Thank you!" And then the card instructed me to turn it over, which I did. On the back of it there was a drawn picture of a deaf-mute person showing me how it is to say "thanks" and how to say "good luck" by the way of the American Single-Hand Manual Alphabet For The Deaf And The Mute. Inside of the folded, light blue card were many little pictures with more instructions. "Hand alphabet used by the Deaf throughout the world. Easy to learn." (*A pause*) And then there were hand diagrams indicating such words as: good, bad, perfect, chance, friend, o.k., right, no good, girl, thanks, boy, and, well, the last two were pictured diagrams for the words: *sweetheart* and *marry*. (*A pause*) Her name was Alice and two months later we were both a sweetheart to each other, and in another two months we both decided to marry each other. (*A pause*) It was heaven for awhile . . .

> (GIGI *and* MIMI *are really interested in what* TODDY *has been telling them*)

TODDY   Then, one day, and it really turned out to be a very bad day for me, I mean when you think about it now, well a real sort of strange miracle took place. My beautiful sexy little Alice, my brand-new beautiful young wife with her sexy-looking body was suddenly involved with an unexplained and very personal and very positive type of wild crazy miracle. Without warning: she was able to hear like the rest of us! Without warning: she was able to talk like the rest of us! (*A pause*) It was a disaster for the both of us. That's right, Gigi and Mimi: it was a horrible disaster for the two of us: my little Alice and me. She didn't like to hear me. She didn't like my voice. Can you believe it, ladies-of-the-night? (*A pause*) And I didn't like her voice either: now that she could speak, well, I didn't want to hear her. It was awful. I wished that she were a mute again. (*A pause*) We could not make love after that. She froze, and so did I. We were two frozen living creatures sleeping side-by-side in our frozen bedroom in our frozen bed in our frozen lives. (*A pause*) It was a devastating thing. It was hell-on-earth. You see, we had been the perfect lovers. It was absolute perfection in that bed, in that bedroom, for my little Alice and me. (*A pause*) Now, well, now, like I said before: it's hell-on-earth . . . a frozen hell in the middle of a frozen earth.

> (*There is a dead silence now. "The Firebird" has just ended on the radio.* TODDY *pulls up his taxicab*)

TODDY   Here we are. You'll have more than enough time. Please: no tips, okay? And no thanks, okay? And no words, okay?

GIGI AND MIMI   But, Toddy . . . ?

TODDY   PLEASE?! OKAY?! NOTHING! ALL RIGHT?!
> (*Dead silence again, except for the snoring of* SPEED. TODDY *gets out of the taxicab. He helps* GIGI *and* MIMI *with* SPEED*: then he also takes out the luggage for them.* SPEED *begins to wake up*)

SPEED   (*Half-awake*)   It's Gucci . . . so be careful . . . you understand cabbie?!
> (TODDY *tries to laugh it off.* GIGI *and* MIMI *offer their hands to* TODDY, *but he pulls away from them. Finally,* GIGI *and* MIMI *give up. They move away with* SPEED *and his luggage.* TODDY *is all alone now. He takes out his pack of bubble-gum and places a piece of it in his mouth; he begins to chew. He laughs strangely when he makes a big*

bubble. Then he reaches in at the front part of his taxicab.
He finds a station on the radio that plays very romantic
instrumental music. Then, very carefully, he goes to the
trunk of his taxicab. He stands there facing the star-
splattered, midnight-blue sky)

TODDY (*Half reciting*) Sexy Sally. Every hot-blooded young
man's dream will surely come true with Sexy Sally. She never
rejects you. She is always ready and always willing. She never
stops waiting for you. She is realistic, no matter how you look
at her. She has a big lucious mouth; soft lips, better-than-
average breasts, and soft enthralling parts from her front as well
as from her back. Sexy Sally: always in favor of you having
your most romantic fantasies come true. Sexy Sally: who also
has a miniature battery power kit so that you can control all of
the tingling, vibrating sensations. Sexy Sally is almost better
than a real woman! She can't talk to you and she can't hear
you, but it doesn't really matter. Because Sexy Sally is only
interested in making love!
    (TODDY *runs back to the taxicab mirror. He fixes himself*
up in it, via his pocket mirror as well. Then he goes back
to the trunk of the taxicab. He unlocks it. Then, very
carefully, he takes out a life-sized-looking bundle
wrapped-up in a pink silk sheet. He removes the sheet. We
see a life-sized, lifelike replica of a naked woman with
everything looking very real about "her." TODDY *holds*
"her" in his arms. He kisses "her")

TODDY (*To "her"*) You're such a bargain, for the blue-collar
working man like me. Fifty-nine ninety-five. (*Laughing*) They
thought I was joking when I said I had a woman in my back
trunk. But what do they know?
    (TODDY *opens up the back door of his taxicab. He places*
the woman's naked replica on "her" back on the back
seat. He blows another bubble with his bubble-gum. He
laughs like an excited little boy)

TODDY (*Whispering*) Oh, Alice, Alice, Alice . . .
    (TODDY *then climbs into the back seat with the naked*
replica of the life-sized, lifelike woman, and closes the
back door behind the two of them, while soft romantic
music plays in the background from the radio)

Curtain
Intermission

The Teaser's Taxi

THE PEOPLE OF THE PLAY
(as they speak)

THE TEASER: an exceptionally handsome youthful-looking man who is probably about 30 years old and who gives a "poetic" first impression of being a sexual-looking modern saint with "perfect" macho charm; he seems both polite, yet strangely rough-tough, and there is also something oddly, almost spiritually funny-wild about him; there is a devilish look in his eyes some of the time and it is most difficult not to be quietly seduced by it; he looks both exciting and immaculate, and he wears a modern-dress black tuxedo while he hacks his taxi-cab, with a white, frilly-looking dress shirt which makes you think of a young poet-nobleman of another time; he is also a beautiful speaker.

CONTESSA DRAKE: a woman who could be 40 or 50—it's hard to tell because of her weird makeup habits—and who is dressed up in all flowing bright red—flaming red!—silk-looking scarf, which is tied loosely around her neck.

SPIKE HORN: a well-dressed young man-in a way—except that there is something "tacky" about his clothes, and he wears lousy shaving cologne, even though he thinks the opposite.

SISTER SERENA: she is probably 30 at the most, and she is truly nervous most of the time, and when we first see her she looks like an older version of a teen-aged country-folk singer.

WHERE THEY ARE

East side, West side, Midtown, all around the Town.

WHEN

Late afternoon, and it is raining outside.

The Teaser's Taxi

We can hear the rain coming down in "gentle buckets," as the lights slowly come up, and then we see THE TEASER's Empty taxicab. Eventually, THE TEASER appears to our right. He is carrying a brightly-striped umbrella, which is very large, and he walks proudly underneath it, guarding himself and his elegant clothes from the rain. He walks all around his taxicab: he is giving it a thorough inspection: he checks all of the tires; he checks all of the door handles from the outside; he takes a dry white cloth and begins to wipe all of the windows. Finally, he closes up his umbrella and climbs into the driver's seat. He dusts everything around him, and he also straightens everything around him: he is a very neat, very meticulous man, to say the least. And now he looks at his reflection in the mirror: he wants to look really good: he fixes the collar of his shirt, smoothes back his hair proudly, and then he brushes off his jacket and pants. He sits back in his seat now, looking bigger than he really is, with his chest and shoulders suddenly taking on a rather large athletic-looking image. He starts up the taxicab now, and as he begins to pull away, he starts to sing out loud to himself, and he has a pretty good voice. He is singing the song: "I've Got The World On A String": a rather rock-pop version of it: he knows all of the lyrics perfectly, and he sings it as though it's a final audition, or something like that.

THE TEASER (*To himself*) Not bad! Not bad at all! Bravo, man, bravo! (*He applauds himself*) You were terrific, Teaser! It looks like you're the guy we're going to give the job to, Teaser! Congratulations, Teaser! We didn't know you had it in you! What a refreshing surprise! What a wonderful discovery! We'll be sending you the contracts in the morning! (*A pause*) And now, it's the next morning, and here I am: signing the contracts, and they're going to bill me as *The Teaser,* and wherever people go from now on, all over the country, from New York to L.A., from Vegas to Atlantic City, they're all going to be listening to the voice of *The Teaser:* One of the great modern pop-rock romantic voices of all time! America will be so proud! And all the rest of the countries around the world will try to find someone to duplicate me, to replace me, but they will all fail at it, because, you see, there's only going to be one me: *The Teaser!*

> (CONTESSA DRAKE *enters, trying to duck the raindrops. She carries a cage-like box with her, which has air holes in it, and which she holds very carefully by the handle*)

CONTESSA DRAKE   Oh, taxi! Taxi! Please stop! My little cat hates the rain! All little cats, and all big cats, too: they all hate the rain! I'm sure you're aware of this fact of the domestic animal kingdom, aren't you, now?! So please: stop for me: and for my little cat: Isadora?!

> (THE TEASER *pulls up for* CONTESSA DRAKE. *He gets out of his taxicab, opens up his umbrella, and escorts his new customer into his taxicab*)

THE TEASER   I'm at your service, lady.

CONTESSA DRAKE   I don't believe it . . .

THE TEASER   You don't believe what?

CONTESSA DRAKE   I don't believe how polite you are . . .

THE TEASER   It's natural with me.

CONTESSA DRAKE   A real honest-to-God-gentleman-taxicab-driver! What a thrill!

> (THE TEASER *begins to drive again, while* CONTESSA DRAKE *fixes herself comfortably in the back seat with her little cat*)

THE TEASER   I'm glad I'm making you happy, lady.

CONTESSA DRAKE   What a pleasure you are! And the way you look?! Well, you look just plain gorgeous!

THE TEASER   Thank you, Lady.

CONTESSA DRAKE   My little cat, Isadora, well, she would just simply love to meet you. She has lots of class too, just like you. I'd let you see her but she's so delicate, you know? I just came from the vets with her. She had stomach pains all day yesterday, and last night she had a terrible headache. It must be terrible for a little cat to have a terrible headache, since they have such little heads in the first place. This morning when we both got up I noticed that she was shivering out of control at the foot of my bed, and so, I immediately made an appointment with Doctor Puss 'N Boots of Animal's Paradise on Kingdom Avenue. Doctor Puss 'N Boots was very kind. He gave Isadora some pills to calm her down. And then he examined her. It turns out that Isadora is having a slight case of a cat's nervous breakdown. But she'll be okay in a few hours, the good doctor told me.

THE TEASER   Holy God . . . !

CONTESSA DRAKE   What's the matter, sir?

THE TEASER   Well, it's just a little hard to believe.

CONTESSA DRAKE   What is?

THE TEASER   Well, everything that you've just told me.

CONTESSA DRAKE   You mean to say that you don't believe me?!

THE TEASER   I didn't say that . . .

CONTESSA DRAKE   But you just implied it!

THE TEASER   No, I really didn't, honest . . .

CONTESSA DRAKE   Yes, you did!

THE TEASER   I didn't!

CONTESSA DRAKE   I hate it when people don't believe me!

THE TEASER   Please, don't get so excited, lady, okay . . . ?

CONTESSA DRAKE   Well, wouldn't you be?!

THE TEASER   But lady . . .

CONTESSA DRAKE   If someone didn't believe you?! You wouldn't feel very good about it, let me tell you? I'm furious with you now! I'm also terribly hurt by you!

THE TEASER   Aw, c'mon, lady . . .

CONTESSA DRAKE   If it weren't raining now I'd get right out of this taxicab and I'd find myself another one to ride in!

THE TEASER   I try, lady, I really try, all of the time . . .

CONTESSA DRAKE   Just take me to Gracie Terrace, that's all I can say!

THE TEASER   What's the number?

CONTESSA DRAKE   I'll show you the building when we get there! Now hurry up!
       (THE TEASER *is rather dejected right now: he feels very upset*)

THE TEASER   I tried, lady . . . I saw you in the rain, and I saw you with your little cat in her little cat's box with the air holes in it . . . I tried, lady . . . I stopped for you immediately, and I jumped out with my umbrella for you, so that I could keep you from getting wet, so that your little cat wouldn't get wet either . . . I tried, lady . . . I really did, you know . . . ?

CONTESSA DRAKE   Well, maybe you try too goddam hard sometimes! Did you ever think of that?!

THE TEASER   No. But now I'm thinking of it.

CONTESSA DRAKE   Good! You should!
       (CONTESSA DRAKE *peeks in at the air holes of the little cat's caged box*)

THE TEASER (*Quietly, more to himself*)   What can you do? All you want is to be good. All you want is for people to be good to you. It's so simple, and it makes so much sense . . .

CONTESSA DRAKE (*To the cat box*)   My poor little Isadora: so white and fluffy: like a little muff to keep my hands warm, like a little pillow to keep my feet warm, like a little white fluffy

ball of fur to lie my head against . . . my poor little Isadora:
we'll be home soon, and then everything will be just fine again,
won't it now: my beautiful poor little Isadora.

THE TEASER (*Quietly, still to himself*)   I didn't count on any of
this happening today. Why can't things work out the way you
want them to work out? The way it only seems right and natural
for them to work out . . . ?

CONTESSA DRAKE (*To the cat box*)   As soon as we get home,
Isadora, I'll give you some more pills, and then, afterwards,
you can take a long nap with me, and then . . .

THE TEASER (*Quietly, still to himself*)   I just don't understand . . .

CONTESSA DRAKE (*To the cat box*)   Well, then we'll get up together, and I'll fix you a nice bowl of pure heavy cream, along
with a little dish of expensive liver pate, okay, my darling little
Isadora?
>   (SPIKE HORN *enters, hailing down the taxicab*)

SPIKE HORN   Hey, taxi, taxi! Give a guy a break, okay?! I've got
this appointment to make! It's very important, man! C'mon?!
Besides, it's raining, and it's screwing-up my clothes and my
hair! C'mon buddy . . . ?!
>   (THE TEASER *pulls up his taxicab*)

CONTESSA DRAKE   What are you doing, driver?!

THE TEASER   What's it look like, lady?

CONTESSA DRAKE   You can't do that!

THE TEASER   Yes, I can.

CONTESSA DRAKE   You can't pick up another fare! You've got
me! And Isadora too!
>   (THE TEASER *gets out of his taxicab with his umbrella and
>   then he escorts* SPIKE HORN *into the back seat, alongside*
>   CONTESSA DRAKE *and the cat box*)

SPIKE HORN   I don't believe you, driver. Man: You're something else. Thanks a lot. I really appreciate it. You have no idea. Listen: I'll tip you big, believe me. (*To* CONTESSA DRAKE) Hi, miss. My name is Spike Horn. What's yours?

CONTESSA DRAKE   This is against the law, driver. I'm going to report you.

SPIKE HORN   He's being a good guy, miss.

CONTESSA DRAKE   It's not right.

SPIKE HORN   I thing it's pretty right to me.

CONTESSA DRAKE   What do you know?! You look cocky and arrogant to me! And what have you got on?! It smells terrible!

SPIKE HORN   I beg your pardon . . . ?

CONTESSA DRAKE   Your after-shaving lotion! It's sickening!

SPIKE HORN   I'm sorry . . .
(THE TEASER *climbs back before the wheel again; he starts* (*off*))

THE TEASER   We'll be dropping the lady and her cat off first . . .

SPIKE HORN   Oh, so you got a cat in there, huh, miss?
(CONTESSA DRAKE *moves the cat box away from him so that he cannot look in it*)

THE TEASER   And then where can I drop you off, buddy?

SPIKE HORN   I'm looking for the piece of paper with the address on it.

CONTESSA DRAKE (*To* SPIKE)   Did you know that I'm royalty?!

SPIKE HORN   No.

CONTESSA DRAKE   Of course you didn't! What would you know about royalty in the first place?!

SPIKE HORN   I guess your right, miss.

CONTESSA DRAKE (*To* THE TEASER)   Did you know that I'm royalty, driver?!

THE TEASER   I could believe it, lady.

CONTESSA DRAKE   Well, you'd better believe it! Both of you! I'm the Contessa Drake!

SPIKE HORN   Contessa Drake, huh? I think I might'uve read about you in the papers. Was your picture on the cover of Midnight last week?

CONTESSA DRAKE   It could have been.

SPIKE HORN   I've never been with a Contessa before.

CONTESSA DRAKE   I'm sure you haven't!

SPIKE HORN   Why are you so unfriendly?

CONTESSA DRAKE   Don't get so personal with me!

SPIKE HORN   Okay.

CONTESSA DRAKE   And why are you dressed that way?! You look like some sort of hired lover, or something like that! And why do you smell that way too?!

SPIKE HORN   That's exactly what I am, miss: a lover who goes out for hire. I'm what you would call a male prostitute. But don't get me wrong. I only go out on hire for women, the opposite sex, because I love women, and so, you see: I'm not a male whore for other men, because other men in bed would not turn me on, except, that, well, maybe, well: if I really needed the money, and I was drunk and not responsible for my actions, well, then it might be a different story. I guess in the end, when you really think about it: sex is sex. And when you can make a few bucks doing it, well, hell, lady: how can a person complain? Right?

CONTESSA DRAKE (*After a pause*)   How much do you charge?

SPIKE HORN   It would be expensive for you.

CONTESSA DRAKE   Why?

SPIKE HORN   Because you're a contessa, that's why.

THE TEASER   It must really be an interesting profession, buddy.

SPIKE HORN   Oh, real interesting, pal.

THE TEASER   How much would you charge someone like the contessa here?

SPIKE HORN   We'd have to talk about it first. It all depends on a whole lot of things.

CONTESSA DRAKE   This is embarrassing.

SPIKE HORN   Never be embarrassed. It's a weakness.

CONTESSA DRAKE   If that's the case: then I'm not embarrassed: because I am not a weak person: I never have been. I am very strong, and very strong-willed.

SPIKE HORN   Oh, yeah?

CONTESSA DRAKE   Yes! For instance: I'll give you an example! Driver?!

THE TEASER   Yes, lady . . . ?

CONTESSA DRAKE   I want you to stop this taxicab of yours, right now! I want you to throw this, this man, this male prostitute out of this taxicab, into the pouring rain, for all I care, because it's not really legal what you've done, by picking him up, when you already had a passenger—*two* passengers: counting my little Isadora here—and if you don't stop and throw him out, this, this sickening-smelling male who has no apparent shame, if you don't command him to get out then I am definitely going to report you to the taxicab authorities, and I'm also going to report you to the police, take my word for it, driver! I'll make

life miserable for you, just the way you're making it miserable
for me! Do you understand?!

(SPIKE HORN *chuckles to himself;* THE TEASER *continues to
drive on*)

CONTESSA DRAKE   Did you hear me, driver?!

SPIKE HORN (*Chuckling still*)   He ain't listening to you, either,

CONTESSA DRAKE   Are you listening to me, driver?!

SPIKE HORN (*Chuckling still*)   He ain't listening to you, either,
Contessa.

CONTESSA DRAKE (*To* SPIKE)   Why don't you shut-up?!

THE TEASER   I didn't hear you, Contessa-whatever-it-is . . .

CONTESSA DRAKE   Drake! Contessa Drake!

THE TEASER   Well, I didn't hear you, Contessa Drake.

CONTESSA DRAKE   You're a liar!

THE TEASER   I don't think I've ever lied in my whole life, at least
I know that I've always tried to tell the truth . . .

CONTESSA DRAKE   I don't believe you for a minute!

THE TEASER   I may have told a little white lie once in a great
while, but that was because . . .

CONTESSA DRAKE   You're so full of it!

SPIKE HORN (*To* CONTESSA DRAKE)   Why don't you let him
finish?

CONTESSA DRAKE   You're full of it too!

THE TEASER   But that was because telling little white lies has to
do with not hurting people . . .

CONTESSA DRAKE   You're just too sweet for words, driver!

SPIKE HORN   You just don't like what he's saying, that's all.

CONTESSA DRAKE   Why don't you take a bath?! Wash off that cheap shaving lotion! Or is it cheap cologne?!

SPIKE HORN   You're really mad at the world, aren't you?

THE TEASER   Like what's-his-name just said: what's your name again, by the way?

SPIKE HORN   Spike Horn.

THE TEASER   Like Spike Horn just said: I didn't hear you, Contessa, and I ain't listening to you, either, Contessa.
    (SPIKE HORN *begins to fumble through all of his pockets*)

CONTESSA DRAKE   What are you doing?!

SPIKE HORN   What's it to you?

CONTESSA DRAKE   You're making me nervous!

SPIKE HORN   Good.

CONTESSA DRAKE   What does that mean?!

THE TEASER (*More to himself*)   I'm just doing what I think is the right thing to do, that's all . . .

SPIKE HORN (*To* CONTESSA DRAKE, *as he still fumbles*)   What does what mean?

THE TEASER (*Still more to himself*)   It has to do with pleasing . . .

CONTESSA DRAKE   I told you that you're making me nervous . . .

SPIKE HORN   So?!

CONTESSA DRAKE   And then you said: *good!*

SPIKE HORN   That's right.

THE TEASER (*Still more to himself*) What's that saying? What's that ancient proverb? I can't remember right now.

CONTESSA DRAKE Why did you say it?! Why did you say: *good?!*

THE TEASER (*Still more to himself*) It has to do with cracking-up, I think . . . this ancient proverb that I'm thaling about . . . cracking-up, that's what it has to do with, I'm certain of it now.

SPIKE HORN I said *good,* Contessa Drake, because I think you should be nervous! I think people should make you nervous because you purposely like to make people nervous, that's why!

CONTESSA DRAKE Do you know something, Spike Horn?

SPIKE HORN What's that, Contessa Drake?

CONTESSA DRAKE I don't like you.

SPIKE HORN That's wonderful! Because I don't like you, either, because you see: you're a fake, that's why!

CONTESSA DRAKE That's exactly why I don't like you: because you're a fake too!
> (SISTER SERENA *enters. She is carrying a medium sized suitcase with her. And the rain now sounds louder than it did before*)

SISTER SERENA Taxi! taxi, taxi! Please, okay, honey?! Will you stop for me?! I'll give you an extra-big tip, take my word for it, okay, honey?!

THE TEASER Of course I'll stop for you! It's pouring rain out there: why wouldn't I stop for you?

CONTESSA DRAKE Don't you dare stop for her, driver!

SPIKE HORN (*Pulling a tiny piece of paper out of one of his pockets*) Oh, here it is! I found it!

SISTER SERENA   Taxi driver, honey, please . . . ?!

CONTESSA DRAKE   Don't you dare, driver!
        (THE TEASER *pulls up for* SISTER SERENA)

SPIKE HORN   Driver: this is where my appointment is: it's at The
    Galeria. You know: that fancy modern place on Fifty-seventh
    Street . . . ?!

SISTER SERENA   Oh, driver: you're such a sweetie-pie!

CONTESSA DRAKE   This is definitely illegal!
        (THE TEASER *gets out of the taxicab with his umbrella; he*
        escorts SISTER SERENA *into the front seat*)

THE TEASER   I hope you don't mind sitting in the front with me?
    It's pretty crowded in the back seat.

SISTER SERENA   Oh, I don't mind at all, driver. I think you're
    wonderful.

THE TEASER   Thank you, lady.

CONTESSA DRAKE   She's no lady! Look at the way she's dressed!

SISTER SERENA   Whose she?!

SPIKE HORN   I don't wanna be late. My appointment, well, she's
    a friend of the mayor's, and, well, she's not only good-looking
    with a terrific-looking body and nice sized boobs, but she also
    likes to pay nice too, and besides liking to pay nice, well, she
    also enjoys it a lot too . . . !

CONTESSA DRAKE   You're so sick!

THE TEASER (*To* SISTER SERENA)   Here, let me take your lug-
    gage . . .

SISTER SERENA   Oh, no, no, no! I need my suitcase, if you don't
    mind?!
        (SISTER SERENA *pulls her suitcase away from* THE TEASER
        as she settles down in the front seat)

SPIKE HORN   Do you want to know something, Contessa Drake?!

CONTESSA DRAKE   No!

SPIKE HORN   That figures.
  (THE TEASER *closes up his umbrella*)

SISTER SERENA (*To* THE TEASER)   I'm going to the Port of Authority Bus Terminal. Anywhere there is fine with me, driver.
  (SISTER SERENA *turns to face* CONTESSA DRAKE *and* SPIKE HORN *in the back seat*)

SISTER SERENA   Hi, everybody back there. My name is Rosemary. But I'm also known as Sister Serena. Well, you'll see . . .
  (THE TEASER *sits back down before the wheel of his taxicab, and then he starts it up again*)

THE TEASER   By the way, uh, Rosemary, uh, Sister Serena: it's not the Port *of* Authority Bus Terminal . . .

SISTER SERENA   What . . . ?!

CONTESSA DRAKE   I want out!

THE TEASER   It's just plain simple: Port Authority . . . without the *of* . . .

SISTER SERENA   Oh . . . ?

CONTESSA DRAKE   Let me outa here!

SISTER SERENA   Thank you for correcting me, driver.

THE TEASER   I just thought I'd mention it to you, that's all.

CONTESSA DRAKE   I WANT OUT!

SPIKE HORN   Hey, driver?! Will you let The Contessa out?! She's getting to be a real royal pain in the ass!
  (CONTESSA DRAKE *slaps* SPIKE HORN *across the face*)

CONTESSA DRAKE   You stink! You fake! You pervert!

SPIKE HORN   LET HER OUT, DRIVER! OTHERWISE I'LL
LAY HER OUT!
(SPIKE HORN *shoves a tight firm fist before* CONTESSA
DRAKE'S *face.* THE TEASER *stops his taxicab real fast.*
CONTESSA DRAKE *jumps out*)

CONTESSA DRAKE   I'm not paying you a cent, driver, because I
don't like you! I'm also not paying you because I don't have the
money! I can get along without you! I can get along without all
of you! Just remember: I'm *the* Contessa Drake . . . and I
own the most beautiful white furry little cat in the world, my
precious Isadora . . . !
(CONTESSA DRAKE *goes running off, leaving the cat-box in
the back seat of the taxicab*)

THE TEASER   She forgot her cat! (*Calling*) Contessa, Contessa!
You forgot your cat! You forgot Isadora!
(SPIKE HORN *rips open the cat box*)

SPIKE HORN   Just like I thought! It's empty!

THE TEASER   What . . . ?!
(SISTER SERENA *is beginning to change her clothes in the
front seat of the taxicab as she opens up her suitcase*)

SPIKE HORN   There's no cat, nowhere!
(SPIKE HORN *lifts the cat box upside-down and shakes it for*
THE TEASER *to see for himself*)

THE TEASER   I don't believe it . . . !

SPIKE HORN   Well, you better baby! She was a big fake, man!
Contessa bullshit! She's nothing, pal! She was putting you on,
buddy! She wanted a free ride, ya' understand?! By the way:
talking about free rides?! Oh, man: wait 'til get in the ole' sack
with this friend of the mayor's. She always pays first, by the
way. Of course those are my rules, my own particular require-
ments. And it's a free ride for me because I get paid for it, you
see? And I can always pretend that she's someone else, that is,
if she doesn't turn me on. You know what ole' Sigmund Freud
once said?! He said that the sexual act of love between two

people usually involves two other people who aren't physically present. Fuck, driver, I can even pretend that I'm making it with you if I want to. She'll never know. And I'll get paid for it too. You know, driver, even though I'm not into men at all—like I said before: I love women—no matter: you're still kinda cute, honest, buddy. Hey, look, I gotta go! I'm five minutes late already.

> (SPIKE HORN *jumps out of the back seat of the taxicab*)

SPIKE HORN   I know I'm gonna see you again, sometime, okay, man? And so, when I do, well, I'll write you out a nice big fat check! I just don't have any cash on me at all right now! Take it easy, baby . . . !

> (SPIKE HORN *goes running off, and, by this time,* SISTER SERENA *is almost fully-dressed in the costume of a Roman Catholic nun, crucifix and all.* THE TEASER *seems to be in a state of quiet shock.* SISTER SERENA *gets out of the front seat of the taxicab*)

SISTER SERENA   (*Holding her suitcase and a papercup*)   Well, that was fast, wasn't it, driver? How do I look?

THE TEASER (*Numbly*)   It's stopped raining . . .

SISTER SERENA   Thank God! Now I can walk to the Port *Of* Authority Bus Terminal. Oh, I know, I know, driver: but I'm so used to calling it by the wrong name.

THE TEASER (*Numbly still*)   Sure . . . Sister . . .

SISTER SERENA   It's Sister Serena.

THE TEASER   Sure . . . Sister Serena, then . . .

SISTER SERENA   Would you like to give help to the poor and the needy: in the name of God?

> (SISTER SERENA *holds the papercup out for* THE TEASER; *he reaches in his pocket and drops a dollar bill into the papercup*)

SISTER SERENA   God bless you, my friend: you're very kind and very generous.

THE TEASER (*Still rather numb*)   Thanks for the blessing, Sister Serena . . .

SISTER SERENA   It's quite all right, driver. We're about the same age, aren't we, now? Well, you know what that means, don't you? It means that we both understand each other in this day and in this age, don't we, now? (*She smiles at him*) I like you a whole lot. I also read cards. I read palms too. I'm not expensive, either. I would like to read your cards sometime; and your palms too. It'll be cheap: because I like you very much. Here's my card-reading card. (*She hands him a card*) And here's my palm-reading card. (*She hands him another card*) Jesus Christ: do I like you! You really have my complete blessings! (*A pause*) Well, I'd better be off for now! I'm way behind schedule. God Almighty: time goes by so fast, doesn't it, now?! And so, blessings from The Blessed Virgin Mary who is also The Immaculate Conception as well. And special blessings from Saint Jude too. He helps all of us whenever we realize what desperate cases we are.
> (SISTER SERENA *holds the papercup out again;* THE TEASER *drops another dollar bill in it*)

SISTER SERENA   God bless you again, my friend.

THE TEASER   Thank you, Sister Serena . . .

SISTER SERENA (*A pause*)   My mother died before I did, and then my father died before I did, too. What else can I tell you, driver? I'm so young yet . . . and yet: I feel so old! (*A pause*) God bless you again, my friend, and yours in Jesus Christ . . . !
> (SISTER SERENA *exits.* THE TEASER's *head falls against the horn of his taxicab. It makes a loud sudden sound. He jumps up in his seat. It is as though he is in a trance: as he sits at his steering wheel*)

THE TEASER (*To himself*)   I don't know, I don't really know. I just want to sing, that's all. I want to be known as *The Teaser*, that's all. A teaser is a nice person, at least I always thought so: a teaser is really innocent and seems to offer nice things: because a teaser is a nice innocent person. He wears beautiful formal clothes when he works for a living, while he dreams of what he would like to be, and he escorts people into his taxicab with his umbrella whenever it's pouring rain outside, and he takes more than one fare at a time: because he's thinking of other people, that's why. (*His head falls on the horn again: the sound of it jolts him back up into a sitting position*) I've always thought in doing what I always thought was right, that's all; it has to do with pleasing; what's that saying? What's that ancient proverb? I can't remember right now. (*A pause*) I know: it has to do with cracking-up, I think . . . this ancient proverb that I'm talking about . . . cracking-up, that's what it has to do with, I'm certain of it now . . . really certain of it now! I could find myself a vacant garage somewhere, and I could close all of the windows of my taxicab, and I could close the doors of the garage, and then I could sit here at my steering-wheel, and I could turn on the motor of my taxicab . . . and then I could just wait until I died . . . ! (*A pause*) But who would care? When you kill yourself you've got to make certain beforehand that people will care after you're gone. (*A pause*) Oh, wait a minute now, wait a minute now! I remember that ancient proverb I've been thinking about. (*He recites very carefully*) "What are the three worse things in the world? Well, the three worse things in the world are: to be in bed and sleep not, to wait for someone who comes not, and to please someone who pleases not." (*A pause; there are tears in his eyes*) I just want to sing, that's all . . . if only one person would listen: I could be happy . . .

(THE TEASER's *face falls on the horn of his steering wheel: it is loud and continuous and it drives us "mad"*)

Curtain

Mr. Tucker's Taxi

THE PEOPLE OF THE PLAY
(*as they speak*)

MR. TUCKER: a man who is going to be 70 years old in a few days, but you would never believe it by looking at him, except for his obvious gauntness, and his ashen paleness; he looks somewhat ailing, naturally, and he certainly does not act old; it is as though his physical sickness has suddenly given him a quiet reinforcing of being alive; his nickname is *Pretzel,* which his wife, Mrs. Tucker, calls him.

MRS. TUCKER: a woman who is going to be 65 years old very soon but who could easily pass for a lovely and youngish 50; her nickname is *Sweets,* which her husband, Mr. Tucker calls her.

BETSY: A sexy-looking woman who is about 25 years old.

LEFTY: A sexy-looking man who is probably in his late 20's.

(NOTE: The parts of BETSY and LEFTY should be played by the actress who plays TAFFY, and the actor who plays TODDY.)

WHERE THEY ARE

Midtown Manhattan, along the Hudson River, and on the George Washington Bridge.

WHEN

Around Noontime

Mr. Tucker's Taxi

MR. TUCKER *is at the wheel of his taxicab and* MRS. TUCKER *is next to him in the front seat. There is a long silence between the two of them. It looks as though the sky outside is rather dismal-looking; it sort of fits the mood that is taking place between* MR. TUCKER *and* MRS. TUCKER.

MR. TUCKER (*Finally*)   I think it's very nice, Sweets.

MRS. TUCKER   What's that, Pretzel?

MR. TUCKER   The fact that you're riding with me.

MRS. TUCKER   Oh, it's nothing.

MR. TUCKER   But it is.

MRS. TUCKER   Okay then.

MR. TUCKER   I wish the sun was out.

MRS. TUCKER   So do I.

MR. TUCKER   It's a funny life.

MRS. TUCKER   I know what you mean.

MR. TUCKER   If only the sun would come out today.

MRS. TUCKER   I think it will.

MR. TUCKER   Well, you usually know what you're talking about.

MRS. TUCKER   Well, so do you, Pretzel.

MR. TUCKER   Ah, Sweets, I love you.

MRS. TUCKER   I love you too.

MR. TUCKER   I love you so much.

MRS. TUCKER   I love you so much too.

> (MR. TUCKER *gives* MRS. TUCKER *a very loving, knowing glance; and then: she returns the same sort of glance to him*)

MR. TUCKER (*After a pause*)   What are we going to do
. . . Sweets?

MRS. TUCKER (*After a pause*)   We're going to keep on going
on . . . just as though everything is normal, that's what we're
going to do. (*Another pause*) We're going to be bright and
cheerful, and we're going to keep right on living, in the way
that we've always done together, ever since our wedding day,
ever since the first time that we both met and it was love at first
sight, without either one of us blinking an eyelash. We both
knew on the spot, didn't we, now? And that spot will always be
there, Pretzel. There's no way in the world that that spot will
ever disappear, do you understand what I'm saying to you
Pretzel?

MR. TUCKER   I understand all of the way, Sweets.

MRS. TUCKER   I know you do.

MR. TUCKER   I understand . . . but at the same time . . . I
don't want to understand. Do you know what I'm saying?

MRS. TUCKER   I know exactly what you're saying.

MR. TUCKER   I feel cheated!

MRS. TUCKER   Please . . . ?!

MR. TUCKER   But I do!

MRS. TUCKER   Oh, please . . . ?!

MR. TUCKER   I'm sorry . . .

MRS. TUCKER   You don't have to apologize. I understand all of
the way.

MR. TUCKER   I know you do. That's what's so wonderful about you, what's so beautiful about you. It's what made me fall in love with you on the spot, the first time that we met, a thousand years ago, even though it seems like only yesterday.

MRS. TUCKER   We've had such a beautiful life together.

MR. TUCKER   We had the best beautiful life together . . .

MRS. TUCKER   Better than anybody else's, believe me . . .

MR. TUCKER   I believe you . . .

MRS. TUCKER   We've got to keep believing, no matter what. . . .

MR. TUCKER   No matter what . . .

MRS. TUCKER   It's the only thing we can do . . .

MR. TUCKER   The only thing we can do . . .

MRS. TUCKER (*After a pause*)   I feel awful! I feel terrible! I feel sick! I feel like it's the end of the world! I can't stand it anymore! I CAN'T . . .

MR. TUCKER   You're losing control, Sweets. You've got to keep calm. You've got to accept certain things . . .

MRS. TUCKER   Why, why, why?! Why do I have to accept certain things?!

MR. TUCKER (*After a pause*)   Because, that's why, because . . . you've got to, that's why. For your own good, do you understand?

MRS. TUCKER   That's just it! I don't! I *don't* understand!

MR. TUCKER   But you've got to.

MRS. TUCKER   No!

MR. TUCKER   You're wrong.

MRS. TUCKER (*After a pause*)   Please forgive me, Pretzel . . . ?

MR. TUCKER   There's nothing to forgive you for. You've done nothing wrong, Sweets.

MRS. TUCKER (*Trying to be calm again*)   I've been awful these last few minutes: selfish and hysterical . . . and . . . just plain awful, Pretzel. I'm so sorry, so *so* sorry.

MR. TUCKER   Everything's going to be alright.

MRS. TUCKER (*After a pause*)   But how can it be . . . ?!

MR. TUCKER (*After a pause*)   I'll tell you what . . .

MRS. TUCKER (*After a pause*)   What . . . ?

MR. TUCKER (*After a pause*)   Why don't you concentrate, Sweets?

MRS. TUCKER   Concentrate . . . ?

MR. TUCKER   Yes, concentrate.

MRS. TUCKER   Concentrate on what?! Concentrate on what's happening to you?! I *can't* bear it, *Pretzel!*

MR. TUCKER   Please . . . ?

MRS. TUCKER   No!

MR. TUCKER   Okay . . . then.
            (*A brief silence*)

MRS. TUCKER   I'm sorry. I don't want you to be mad at me.

MR. TUCKER   I'm not mad at you.

MRS. TUCKER   I'm glad you're not.

MR. TUCKER   I guess the reason it's so gloomy outside is because it looks like it's going to rain. I mean, will you just take a look at the way the color of the sky is changing? It's turning into dark grey and dark yellow.

(MRS. TUCKER *looks up at the sky from the taxi window*)

MRS. TUCKER   It's really weird-looking, isn't it?

MR. TUCKER   It looks like the end of the world.

MRS. TUCKER (*After a pause*)   It is . . . *the end of the world!*

MR. TUCKER   Now, c'mon: don't get into it.

MRS. TUCKER   Oh . . . really?! Well, it's very hard not to get into it!

MR. TUCKER   I know, I know . . . ! But try not to. For your own sake. Not my sake, but for your own sake. Do you understand what I'm trying to tell you, Sweets . . . ?

MRS. TUCKER (*Suddenly*)   Oh, my God . . . ! Look . . . !

MR. TUCKER   What's wrong?!

MRS. TUCKER   Nothing's wrong! That's the whole thing! Look!
(*There is a sudden burst of the rays of the sun: it floods the whole area very slowly, but very definitely: it is very warm and very bright*)

MR. TUCKER (*Looking out*)   That's really strange . . . it's really weird-looking! Where did it come from?! I don't think I've ever seen the sun so bright!

MRS. TUCKER   It's like a miracle!
(*But then, suddenly, the sun goes back out again*)

MR. TUCKER   Well, that's that. It's all over. It didn't last very long, did it?

MRS. TUCKER   I know. But I guess it was better than nothing at all.

MR. TUCKER   Maybe we shouldn't have noticed it. Maybe we shouldn't have said anything about it to each other.

MRS. TUCKER   Maybe. But it really did seem like a miracle . . . don't you think, Pretzel?

MR. TUCKER   It sure did.
 (*Silence again*)

MRS. TUCKER (*Finally*)   It's not too busy today.

MR. TUCKER   So far it's not. But that's the way it is sometimes. It'll pick up all of a sudden. That's the way it usually happens.

MRS. TUCKER   I'm sort of glad. It gives us more time to ourselves. It gives us more of a chance to talk to each other without being interrupted.

MR. TUCKER   You know: when I get to Heaven . . .

MRS. TUCKER   Don't talk like that!

MR. TUCKER (*Going on*)   First of all: I figure I've been a pretty good human being . . . a nice sort of man, a decent guy in the long run . . . and so I think I'll be meeting Saint Peter at those golden gates way up there . . .

MRS. TUCKER (*Trying to be calm*)   I wish you wouldn't . . .

MR. TUCKER (*Continuing, as though he is rehearsing by himself now*)   I'll say to Saint Peter: yes, I'm Thomas Tucker . . . Mr. Tucker . . . and I'm married to—or rather: I was married to—Teresa Tucker . . . Mrs. Tucker . . . but we always called each other by our nicknames. She called me *Pretzel* because I loved eating pretzels all of the time, even without the beer, even when I wasn't watching television. It was always my favorite in-between snack whenever I was awake. And I always called her *Sweets* simply because she loved sweets, all of the time: she would practically live on candy and pastries, but mainly on candy. And she was lucky too, Saint Peter, because she always kept herself real slim, despite all of that sugar in her body. We loved each other very much, and so, we called each other by the names of other things that we loved so very much: Pretzel and Sweets. (*He sighs*) I think if I just tell Saint Peter that little story alone, well, he'll let me pass by those golden gates without any doubt in his mind at all.
 (**MRS. TUCKER** *tries to smile a little bit. Then she takes a*

bag of pretzels out of her handbag. She hands the bag of pretzels to MR. TUCKER)

MRS. TUCKER Here you are, Pretzel.

MR. TUCKER Thank you, Sweets.

MRS. TUCKER Enjoy them . . .

MR. TUCKER I know I will . . .
(MR. TUCKER *then reaches into a paperbag at his side; he pulls out a small white box of candy, and then he hands it to* MRS. TUCKER)

MRS. TUCKER Candy, right?

MR. TUCKER Right, Sweets. Coconut bon-bons. All different colors. They're supposed to be delicious: the best ones in town. Some guy makes them near the City Squire Inn, all alone in his little candy store.
(MRS. TUCKER *opens up the little white box*)

MRS. TUCKER (*Looking happy*) Oh, Pretzel, they're all so beautiful-looking! Thank you so much.
(MR. TUCKER *begins to eat pretzels, while* MRS. TUCKER *begins to eat bon-bons. They seem at least half-contented. Then, suddenly, the sun comes out again, and it's even brighter than before.* MR. TUCKER *and* MRS. TUCKER *are very pleased as it happens: we can tell: they both smile at each other. Then without any warning:* BETSY *appears on the scene. She is frantic as she tries to hail* MR. TUCKER'S *taxicab down*)

BETSY Taxi, taxi, *taxi!* Please . . . ?! I've got to go to a hospital! TAXI . . . !
(MR. TUCKER *pulls up before* BETSY *as she climbs into the back seat of his taxicab*)

MR. TUCKER What's the matter, miss?!

BETSY Take me to the nearest hospital, that's all! I've been raped! It happened just a little while ago! It was my fault, in a way . . . I should have been more discreet . . . I should have realized why he came here! I went up to his room in The Americana, something I should never, ever have done. Take me to Roosevelt Hospital, fast! I know the people there, if that's going to mean anything! He was my half-brother, but there's no blood relationship, not really. But that's a long story. I won't go into it now. The main thing is: *I can't have a baby!* I've got to see a doctor fast! I don't believe in abortions, you see?! If I get there in time, well, maybe some doctor will be able to do something for me, before it's too late! Maybe, if I get there in time, he'll know what to do before I'm really pregnant! Oh, I'm so dumb about things like this! And I don't want to have to have an abortion! But I also don't want to have a baby! Hurry, driver, please, hurry . . . ?!

MR. TUCKER   I'm trying, miss.

BETSY   Try harder, please?! I have lots of money! I'll give you a big tip! I'll give you five dollars if you get me there in time! I don't want an abortion! And I don't want a baby, either! Please?! I'll give you ten dollars instead!

MR. TUCKER   I'm doing my best, miss.

MRS. TUCKER (*To* BETSY)   You're very nervous, miss. Maybe I can help you to relax. What's your name?

BETSY   Betsy. Who are you?!

MRS. TUCKER   I'm Sweets. And my husband here: is Pretzel.

BETSY   Sweets?! Pretzel?! What's going on here?!

MR. TUCKER   I'm taking you to Roosevelt Hospital, that's what's going on!

BETSY   You're married to each other?!

MRS. TUCKER   That's right.

BETSY   Do you always travel like this together? In the front seat like that?!

MRS. TUCKER   Only lately, Betsy.

BETSY   It's weird. But it's also nice . . .

MRS. TUCKER   Thank you, Betsy.

MR. TUCKER   So you wanna make sure you don't have to have an abortion, huh?

BETSY   The thought of it horrifies me. I have enough problems. I can't deal with new ones.

MR. TUCKER   And you also don't wanna have a baby . . . ?

BETSY   That would be another problem, believe me!

MR. TUCKER   Have you ever had any children before, Betsy?

BETSY   None!

MRS. TUCKER   Then you don't really know . . . ?

BETSY   I don't want to know! Besides, I have an idea! And besides: I'm also too young to be tied down. I have a whole future ahead of me. And besides: I don't think I'd be a very good mother right now. And besides: I'm not married, which means I'm not in love, which means there's no reason for me to have a baby right now. Do you both understand?!

MRS. TUCKER   Pretzel and me been married for a very long time: a very long and *very* happy time. We don't have children. God knows: we wanted children. We tried . . .

MR. TUCKER   Don't . . .

MRS. TUCKER   (*Going on*)   We had two kids. The first one was a boy, and he died. Then we had another kid: a girl. She also didn't last. (*A pause*) But we did! Pretzel and me, well, we both lasted! It was hard and it was horrible, but we didn't give up. The little boy died before he was seven months old. An unusual disease that's very rare. (*Mocking laughter*) I always thought that things that were rare also meant that they were precious and beautiful: like rare paintings and rare jewels and rare works of literature. Well, let me tell you, Betsy! We were both fooled, let me tell you! What's so precious and what's so beautiful about a rare disease that kills your first born, your son, *our* son?!

MR. TUCKER   Is this making you feel okay, Sweets? Saying all of this?

MRS. TUCKER   Yes, I think it is.

MR. TUCKER   Then go ahead, Sweets.

MRS. TUCKER   What about you, Pretzel?

MR. TUCKER   If it's making you feel okay, then it's making me feel okay too.

BETSY   It's all very interesting, and everything else: but I've got to get to a hospital before it's too late!

MR. TUCKER   We're getting there, Besty . . .
     (*The bright sun dies away again, very fast, almost as if someone merely turned it off*)

MRS. TUCKER   Did you see that?! Did you see the way the sun just simply disappeared again?! As though someone pressed a button and turned it off . . .

BETSY   Well, it's not a very happy day for me, so why should the sun be shinning in the first place? That would be too easy. That wouldn't make sense, because when it rains it pours . . . and well . . . it might as well be pouring right now. Because it's certainly pouring for me right now!

MRS. TUCKER   Let me tell you something, Betsy . . .

BETSY   Just tell me that we'll get to the hospital on time, that's all!

MR. TUCKER   We're almost there.

BETSY   Why is every goddam light a goddam red light?!

MR. TUCKER   That's the way it is sometimes . . .

BETSY   It's nerve-wrecking . . .

MRS. TUCKER   I started to tell you before, Betsy: let me tell you something. Remember . . . ?

BETSY   I remember. But I don't have the time to listen. And just remember what I said back to you . . . Sweets! I told you to just tell me that we'll get to the hospital in time, remember? I love kids, and I love parents, but right now I'm not ready for any of that. I was raped, and don't either one of you forget it, either!

MRS. TUCKER   But you did say that some of it was your fault.

BETSY   It was. But most of it was his. He always wanted me, my half-brother, down in Baton Rouge. I was scared to death of him because I thought we both were related by blood, because he was my father's son by another marriage. But then I found out that he had been adopted by my father and my father's second wife. My father's second wife couldn't have babies.

MRS. TUCKER   Well, let me tell you . . .

MR. TUCKER   She doesn't want to hear, Sweets. Can't you tell? She's hysterical.

BETSY   Well, you'd be hysterical too, if you were in my situation!

MRS. TUCKER   Here. Have a bon-bon.
        (MRS. TUCKER *offers the box of candy to* BETSY)

BETSY (*Looking*)   They look beautiful. But how can I eat candy right now?!
        (MR. TUCKER *offers his bag of pretzels to* BETSY)

MR. TUCKER   Have a pretzel then.

BETSY   Don't you two people understand?! How can I think about eating candy and pretzels at a time like this?! I could be pregnant, you know?! Oh, my God: the thought of it makes me cringe with fear! I'm so worried! Could it be too late?! I'm dumb about things like this! I told you both that before, didn't I?! Well, I'm dumb about things like this because I'm forcing myself to be dumb right now. I'm concentrating on a miracle, that's what I'm concentrating on! I'm praying to God that I'm not pregnant, that's all . . . and it's dumb of me, I know . . . but why couldn't it be true, right?! I mean: anything is possible! On television, in the papers: we're always reading something that has to do with people and things that we would have believed would have been impossible. (*A pause.*) I'm trying not to cry, but it's becoming very hard for me. So, please: get me to that goddam hospital before I go insane right here in the back of your cab, please?!

MR. TUCKER We're almost there.

BETSY Almost is not enough, goddammitt!

MRS. TUCKER Don't you dare talk to my husband that way, do you hear me?! And let me tell you what I tried to tell you before . . .

BETSY I don't wanna hear it!

MRS. TUCKER I was going to tell you how dumb you were, how dumb you really are! Of course you've already admitted that to yourself, and you admitted it to us too. Well, that's just what you are: you're absolutely dumb! Pretzel and me, well, we just simply lived for each other after we lost our little son and our little daughter. We were afraid to take another chance after that. Maybe we were both wrong then. Maybe we're both sorry for it now. Maybe we were dumb, just like you, Betsy. What I'm telling you is to take the chance . . . take the chance and have the baby, do you understand what I'm trying to tell you? Besides, you've got to face facts, honey . . . *one fact,* really: the chances are that you're going to have a baby, and that's all there is to it.

BETSY I think you're terrible for telling this! It's none of your business! I shouldn't have told either one of you anything about it! I don't care what you say, and I'm not going to believe what you think!

(LEFTY *appears real fast. He carries a small suitcase with him. He tries to be calm and collected and "invisible" as well)*

MRS. TUCKER   You're a sorry case, a very, *very* sorry case!

BETSY   Get me to that hospital, driver!

MR. TUCKER   That's what I'm doing, miss.

BETSY   Then why aren't we moving?!

MR. TUCKER   Because we got another red light, that's why.

BETSY   Oh, I'm going crazy, I know I am!
(LEFTY *suddenly rushes towards the taxicab. He swings open the back door and jumps into the back seat with* BETSY, *and then, before any of them can say anything, he pulls out a revolver)*

LEFTY   No one move, see?! (*He waves the gun at all of them*) If anyone makes one move I'll kill you, each and everyone of you! (*To* BETSY) Move over near the window on your side, and stay there! (BETSY *obeys*) All right now! Cabbie, I want you to be cool and calm and collected, see? And the same goes for you, lady, you understand? (*He pokes the back of* MRS. TUCKER's *head with his gun*) As soon as the light changes I want you to head up along the Hudson River, cabbie, and then I want you to go all the way up to the George Washington Bridge, and I want you to drive over the bridge until we're in New Jersey, and then when we get there I'll give you more directions, okay? All right, the light just changed, so start moving, cabbie. (*To* BETSY) Maybe you should sit closer to me, come to think of it. Look more friendly. C'mon, sit closer to me or I'll blow your sexy brains out! (BETSY *moves closer to him*) Thatta girl. What's your name?

BETSY (*Horrified*)   Betsy . . .

LEFTY   Like Betsy Ross, huh? The lady who made the American flag.

BETSY   I was on my way . . . to the hospital . . . ! Please . . . ?!

LEFTY Shut-up! (*To* MR. TUCKER) What's your name, cabbie? I figure we might as well make this all as friendly as possible. You with me?

MR. TUCKER I'm with you.

MRS. TUCKER I call him Pretzel. He's my husband.

LEFTY You wait your turn, lady. I didn't ask you yet.

MR. TUCKER It's a nickname: Pretzel. It's what most people call me.

LEFTY Okay, Pretzel: good enough. (*To* MRS. TUCKER) And what's yours, lady? It's your turn now.

MR. TUCKER I call her Sweets. She's my wife.

LEFTY Let her speak for herself, man!

MRS. TUCKER My husband's right. I'm called Sweets.

BETSY I'm getting sick . . .

LEFTY Shut up!

BETSY Oh, God . . . !

LEFTY I told you to shut up!
　　　　(BETSY *closes her eyes and clutches at her stomach.* MR. TUCKER *tries to be calm, and so does* MRS. TUCKER)

MR. TUCKER Where are we going in New Jersey?

LEFTY I told you I'll let you know when we get there.

MR. TUCKER You're the boss.

LEFTY I sure am, buddy! I'm gonna be the boss from now on for all time, see? I just robbed this bank, see? and this little suitcase here is filled with money, lots and lots of money, at least a hundred thousand dollars, see? Do you realize what a man can do with a hundred thousand dollars? He can become the boss, that's what he can do. He can be free to do what he wants to do. I want to be free enough to be the boss forever. I wanna boss other people around, that's all. I used to have an inferiority complex. It was real bad, let me tell you. Well, the only way you can cure an acute case of feeling inferior is by going in the other direction, see? What you do is you strive for a superiority complex, you understand? I was an orphan and I never knew who my fucking father was, which means, of course, I never knew who my fucking mother was, either. Fuck 'em! Fuck 'em both, wherever they are! But I hope they're both nowhere, see?! I hope they both croaked a long time ago, and I hope to God that they really suffered horrible deaths, too! (*A pause*) I'm gonna spend the rest of my life making this hundred grand multiply into millions, you all just wait and see. And then I'm really gonna spend the rest of my life being the boss, bossing everybody around. It's going to be such a wonderful trip! Such a grand and such a glorious trip, a real superior adventure. And God knows: we all want that: we all want to have superior adventures. You know something? Most people have inferiority complexes. Only a chosen few, like myself, for instance, finally wind up with very special kind of superiority complex. (*A pause*) Oh, by the way, everybody: my name is Lefty. It's nickname too, because I write with my left hand. Lefty, that's me. I played ball with my left hand too. Well, look: here's proof of my name: I'm holding my gun with my left hand. I even take a leak with my left hand. I've heard that Abraham Lincoln was left-handed. That says something, doesn't it now? I mean it says something about me. But he was a dumb bastard, really. I mean, he got himself killed by some lousy actor with a rotten inferiority complex. (*He looks out the window*) It's too bad that the sun isn't out right now. You know why? Because the Hudson River really loks beautiful when the sun is shining down on it, it really does, take my word for it. (*A pause*) Hey! We're not far away. I can see the George Washington Bridge in the distance. It's my favorite bridge, by the way. (*A pause*) Hey, Pretzel! Sweets! I'm Lefty! Hey! Betsy Ross here! I'm Lefty! (*Dead silence*) Aw, shit! Maybe it's better you all keep your mouths shut. But let me tell you all something else too. When we pay the toll on the George Washington Bridge I want all of us to be talking, you understand? And a very friendly-like too. I don't want anybody getting suspicious, okay? (*A pause*) So you two up front are for real, huh? I mean you're really man and wife. That's really nice. Do you ride with your husband all the time, Sweets?

MRS. TUCKER   Only lately . . .

LEFTY   Why only lately? Trying to save a marriage, or something? Is your marriage on the rocks, or something like that?

MR. TUCKER   We're okay . . .

LEFTY   Yeah? Well, you don't look so okay? What's happening with the two of you? I wanna hear, okay?
>   (MR. TUCKER *looks at* MRS. TUCKER; *he tries to smile at her; and then she tries to smile back at him.* BETSY *continues to keep her eyes closed and clutches at her stomach still*)

BETSY (*Mumbling*)   Oh, God, . . . help us . . . help me!

LEFTY (*To* BETSY)   Shut up! (*To* MR. *and* MRS. TUCKER) I'm all ears. Start talking. Both of you.

MRS. TUCKER   Do you really want to listen?

LEFTY   Yep. It'll pass the time away. It'll make us all less nervous too. So, g'wan, Sweets. Let's hear from you.

MRS. TUCKER (*After a pause*)   Our marriage was never really on the rocks. We're not about to save a marriage because there's no need for that. There never has been.

MR. TUCKER   You know . . . Lefty?

LEFTY   What?

MR. TUCKER   You can shoot me dead if you want to. It wouldn't phase me one bit. I'm just concerned about my wife, that's all. And my passenger, Betsy, that's all.

LEFTY   Don't give me any of that hero bullshit.

MR. TUCKER   I'm not.

MRS. TUCKER   He's right. He's not.

LEFTY   It's all fucking bullshit! I hate fucking bullshit artists who also think they're fucking heros!

MR. TUCKER   But I'm not a bullshit artist who thinks he's a hero. (*A fast pause*) You see . . . Mr. Lefty . . . It's . . .

LEFTY   No *Mr.* Lefty, man! It's just *plain* Lefty!

MR. TUCKER   Okay, plain Lefty . . .

LEFTY   Knock it off, wise-ass! Otherwise I'll kill you before the day is over with! Now g'wan!

MR. TUCKER   All Right, Lefty. (*A fast pause*) The reason that my wife rides in the front seat of my taxicab these days is very simple . . .

MRS. TUCKER   Don't tell him . . . !

MR. TUCKER   It's all right, Sweets, honest-to-God it is. The reason that Sweets rides in the front seat with me these days is because I ain't gonna live much longer. Yep, that's a fact. I know it, and Sweets knows it too. The doctor told Sweets first, and she kept it a secret from me for a long time now. But I could tell. Finally, I got the doctor to tell me . . . and eventually, well, I got Sweets to tell, me too . . .

MRS.   TUCKER   (*Her   hands   to   her   mouth*)   Oh . . . Pretzel . . . !

MR. TUCKER   It's not really that bad, Lefty. It's just a matter of a month or two at the most. It's a case of me and Sweets just trying to be together as much as possible. It's just a case of me keeping as busy as always, as though nothing is going to happen. You see, life goes on—and it should!—even if you know your days are definitely marked. Reality is what I'm facing, and Sweets is facing it with me. It's probably harder for her than it is for me. Actually, I feel sort of lucky. I mean I'm still able to hack a cab with the knowledge that I'm not going to be around anymore within the next couple of months. (*A pause*) Do you get the picture now, Lefty? I'm not a hero. No bullshit about me. You can shoot me dead right now. No sweat off my back. Just leave Sweets alone. And the girl too. That's all I'm saying.

    (BETSY *opens her eyes*)

MRS. TUCKER (*Trance-like*)   And let me go further, Lefty! You can kill me too, because I ain't gonna live much longer, after Pretzel is gone! So that's what you gotta do, *Mister* Lefty! (*Out of the "trance"*) You go ahead, and pull that trigger! I dare you, *Mister* Lefty! You'd be doing us a favor, both of us, believe me! You get me in the head! And you get Pretzel in the head too! That way, well, that way: we can go together: at the same time, *Mister* Superiority Complex! Just two bullets! And you can make two people awfully happy! My God! You can really be *the boss* you've been talking about! You have the chance to *boss* the lives right out of us, right now, this very instant! *I dare you!*

(*Dead silence*)

BETSY (*Finally*)   I don't believe any of this . . .

LEFTY   Shut up!

MRS. TUCKER (*To* LEFTY)   I said I dare you, *Mister* Lefty!

LEFTY   Shut up!

MR. TUCKER   Sweets and me: well, we're both daring you, *Mister* Lefty.

LEFTY   Shut up! All of you! Shut up, or I'll blow all of your brains out! (*Looking out the window*) We're almost on the George Washington Bridge! Be friendly, everybody! Be friendly, if you know what's good for you, especially when we get to the other side, when we're paying the bridge toll! You said you were going to some hospital! What are you doin'?! Are you kicking the bucket too?!

BETSY (*Very fast*)   I was raped, and I don't want to have the baby, and I don't want to have an abortion, either! But now it's all too late, because of you!

LEFTY   I think you're all goin' bananas! But let me tell you something, Betsy Ross! If you're gonna have a kid, well, you go ahead and you have that kid, and don't you desert that kid, either! If I knew that you'd desert that kid of yours, well, baby, I'd blow your brains out right now! You understand what I'm trying to tell you?! Don't make that kid of yours an orphan! Don't fuck him up—or her up—for the rest of their lives! You understand?! I hope you're gonna have a kid so that you'll keep it, and take care of it, and, most of all . . . *love* it! You understand?! (*Looking out*) We're on the George Washington Bridge now! Be cool! Everybody be nice and cool, or else!

BETSY   I feel so terrible . . .

LEFTY   Shut up! Snuggle up to me! Make believe you're my ole' lady.

      (LEFTY *hides the gun, and then he forces* BETSY *to sit closer to him*)

MR. TUCKER   I dare you!

LEFTY   Shut up!

MRS. TUCKER   Yes! We *both* dare you!

LEFTY   I said to shut up!

BETSY   I feel so horrible . . .

LEFTY   SHUT UP!

MR. TUCKER (*Suddenly, as if in pain*)   It's really funny, Betsy . . .

MRS. TUCKER   What's the matter, Pretzel?!

MR. TUCKER (*In pain now*)   Well, Sweets . . . I'm beginning to feel horrible too, just like Betsy, I'm feeling sick and terrible and horrible, just like our little Betsy back there . . . ! I don't know . . . what's wrong! Oh, Sweets! Watch out, Sweets! Don't get hurt, Sweets! It's getting worse! And it's getting dark Sweets . . . ?!

      (MR. TUCKER *slumps over the steering-wheel, moaning and groaning, and then he dies. The taxicab goes crashing off against the steel of the George Washington Bridge, and* MRS. TUCKER *and* BETSY *let out long screeching screams, as the two of them, along with* MR. TUCKER *and* LEFTY, *are thrown all over the area, like scattered rag dolls. There is a lot of racket consisting of crashing metal and smashing glass. The suitcase belonging to* LEFTY *flies wide-open and all of the hundred-thousand dollars in bills goes flying all over the stage like big green-and-white paper confetti. We hear horns honking now. And then there is dead silence. TABLEAU: the four bodies lying still, all sprawled out in quiet poses. Eventually only one of them stirs. It is* BETSY. *She slowly lifts herself up and begins to look around. She is shocked. She stands on her knees. Then always on her knees, she begins to move towards the bodies of the other three. She touches* MR. TUCKER *first, and then she goes to* MRS. TUCKER *and touches her; finally, she goes to* LEFTY *and touches him, always on her knees. She clutches at her stomach for a moment or two.* BETSY *looks up at the sky. The sun begins to come out again. It is very bright. In the distance we can hear the horns honking again, very briefly. Then dead silence again.* BETSY *remains on her knees, in the middle of the stage, with the three dead bodies of* MR. TUCKER, MRS. TUCKER *and* LEFTY *scattered still-like about her. The sun grows remarkably bright, and* BETSY *is both crying and half-smiling)*

Slow Dim-Out

Curtain

RUSTY AND RICO AND LENA AND LOUIE

(TWO ONE-ACT PLAYS)

For The Women:

Stephanie Gordon
Maggie Burke
JoAnn Tedesco
and
Mimi Matera

RUSTY AND RICO AND LENA AND LOUIE was first presented the I.R.T. (Impossible Ragtime Theatre), New York City, on May 5th, 1978, with the following cast:

RUSTY, LENA .... *Maggie Burke*

RICO, LOUIE .... *Justin Deas*

Directed by John Shearin

Sets by Tom Warren

Lighting by Curt Ostermann

Costumes by Margo LaZaro

Rusty and Rico

THE PEOPLE OF THE PLAY
(*as they appear*)

RUSTY: a breathtakingly beautiful New York Jewish hooker who wears a long golden-blonde wig that falls lushly all the way down to her willowy waist, and who also wears extra-high gleaming white leather boots that go all the way up to her nice knees with extra-high heels on them, and, to match them—of all things!— pure white lady-like gloves that go all the way up to her erotic elbows.

RICO: an awfully appealing politician who is in his late 20's which makes him probably about ten years younger than RUSTY, who is half-Irish and half-Italian, and who wears very ultra-modish clothes which look awfully good with his wild dark hair, and who also wears extra-heeled shoes so that he won't look shorter than RUSTY whenever she is wearing hers.

WHERE THEY ARE

RUSTY and RICO: Central Park in Manhattan.

WHEN

RUSTY and RICO: well past midnight during the present time.

Rusty and Rico

When the lights come up we see RUSTY *and we hear music: the music is coming from a small transistor radio—actually, it's not that small: but a rather obvious prop belonging to* RUSTY—*and the music is "The Love I Lost," sung by Harold Melvin and the Blue Notes, and* RUSTY *is half-singing with them and half-dancing too. There are flashing city light effects in the beaming night-blue background. But then, slowly, the effects go away. It is like we are suddenly in the quiet country at nighttime; maybe once in awhile we hear the honking of a car horn in the far distance. We are in the middle of Sheep's Meadow now, in Central Park. We can see the twinkling lights of the buildings on all the three possible sides, along with the twinkling stars in the midnight-blue sky.*

RUSTY (*To the audience*) When I was a little girl—and that wasn't too long ago, either, let me tell you—I wanted to be just like: Anne Bancroft and Geraldine Page and Colleen Dewhurst, and, of course: Kim Stanley. Now that I'm past being a little girl—by the way: when I say I was a little girl I'm counting all the way up until after eighteen years of age—well, anyway: when I became a big girl, which is what I am right now: I changed a whole lot, or maybe that word is *grew:* maybe I *grew* a whole lot: that's a good thing to think about, by the way: the difference between changing in a person and growing in a person. Well, when I became this big girl that I am right now I wanted to be like Bella Abzug and Ella Grasso and Margaret Chase Smith and Shirley Chisolm, and, of course: Gloria Steinem: with the creativeness of, yes: Jane Fonda, and, finally, wrapping it all up: with the personality of Ms. Patti Hearst Herself. But what happened?! Well, I wish the hell I goddam knew! (*A pause*) Here I am: all alone in the middle of Sheep's Meadow in Central Park. I've just finished hustling my ass in the back shadows of the Waldorf-Astoria, no less, hustling my anxious ass for whatever amount of money seems in any way reasonable and in any way realistic to me these hard horny habitual nights of such half-hellish honey-pot hooking. It's really something: life! It's really something: the process of living! I mean: it's strange and wild and sometimes it's even wonderful! I mean to say now: do you know whose staying in the Waldorf-Astoria Towers right now at this very moment? The Shah of Iran, The Queen of the Netherlands, that Princess from England, Cassius Clay Himself, Richard M. Nixon incognito, that's right, and Mamie Eisenhower too, all at the exact same time, and all of them using the same water that I use, and breathing the same air that I breathe, and maybe listening to the same music that I'm listening to, and probably even using the same brand of toilet paper that I use too. Well, anyway: there I was, a little while ago: trying to make men as happy as possible so that in turn I'll be as happy as possible, which, in turn, means *I am* happy, because *I am* free! Free because of the money I can make: on my back and on my knees and with my lips, and, well, you know: all of the other blessed parts of my blessed ''passing-through-time-and-space''body and figure: eventually on my way to Heaven: just like all the rest of us. I'm really not complaining, you know? It's really not bad at all: but that's because I am completely in love! I am in love with a man who is ten years younger than I am. So you see: it's really a very special kind of love. The best! I never thought in a million years that it would happen to me like this: but it did: I am madly, hopelessly, desperately, beautifully in love: pure sheer mere love! And just wait until you meet this younger man that I love, the man that I am in love with so much!

> (RICO *enters through the audience, waving to everybody, shaking hands, but never saying anything: he just always smiles. When he reaches the stage area, he stops, takes a long loving look at* RUSTY *and then puts on a pair of large sunglasses*)

RUSTY Hello, Rico.

RICO How you doing, Rusty?

RUSTY I'm doing fine: now that you've come.
> (RUSTY *stops her dancing and turns off her transistor-radio*)

RICO No, don't.

RUSTY Don't what?

RICO Don't stop dancing and don't turn off the music.

RUSTY   Why?

RICO   Because I liked the music and I liked the way you were dancing and just simply because I want to dance with you, that's why, Rusty.
(RICO *takes the transistor-radio from* RUSTY *and turns it back on: Elton John is singing: "Philadelphia Freedom."* RICO *begins to dance, and so, quite happily:* RUSTY *joins in with him*)

RUSTY   I hope you won't be recognized. I hope you won't get in trouble.

RICO   I'm beginning to feel free again, Rusty. I'm beginning to feel that I can still run for things, be a truly free politician, run for City Councilman again, and win as City Councilman again. (*He turns to face the audience; then, like a very appealing politician he still manages to dance, he addresses them loudly but very nicely*) My name is Rico and I'm half-Italian and I'm half-Irish . . .

RUSTY   And some people . . . most people, well, they think that you're an awfully appealing politician too!

RICO   Just the way that some people . . . most people, well, they think that you're an awfully appealing hooker too!

RUSTY   Why thank you very much: Mr. City Councilman!

RICO   Why, my God, Rusty! You're the most breathtakingly beautiful New York Jewish hooker in all of the boroughs!

RUSTY   You're always such a delicious dream to have around, Rico.

RICO (*To the audience*)   Help keep our district a place for people. Not hamburgers or Medicaid mills. Re-elect City Councilman Rico Roma, Tuesday, November Fifth, between Six A.M. and Nine P.M., your devoted and dutiful, and yes, *delicious* dream, and yes, your *delicious* and ultra damn dashing *deliciously young in heart-and-soul*—and penis too!—Democrat/Liberal candidate of the immediate now and the forever future! (*He goes back to dancing and facing* RUSTY) So what if I'm in love with you?! So what if you're the first real woman I've ever been

so downright madly in love with?! So what if I'd die for you
because I love you so much?! My God! They should know it,
all of the people should know it! They should know that they're
voting for a real human being who feels, who feels just the way
they all feel deep down inside. Don't you think I'm right: my
ravishing raunchy, ole' reliable, gorgeous, ravishingly beautiful Rusty?!

(RUSTY *turns off the transistor-radio immediately. They
both stop dancing now*)

RUSTY   If you really mean all of that, darling-Rico, then take off
those expensive shades of yours so that they can all see you, so
that they can all tell who you are, so that they can trust you and
believe in you, and believe in what you say and preach and in
what you do. Do it, Rico Roma, if you really mean what you
say, if you really believe in the heart and the soul first, and if
you really believe in real true honest never-ending *freedom!*

(*There is a short pause. Finally,* RICO *takes off his sunglasses and throws them away*)

RICO   Okay . . . !

RUSTY   I love you more than I ever thought I could love you,
Rico.

RICO   Same goes for me in relation to you, Rusty.
(*They both shake hands very firmly; and then the hand-
shaking turns into a firm hug and then, finally, into a fast
kiss on the lips*)

RUSTY   We're so lucky.

RICO   I never felt lucky until the day that I met you.

RUSTY   I was just going to say the same thing: I never felt lucky
until the day that I met you.

RICO   Let's take a little quiet secret walk, okay? Holding hands,
all right?

RUSTY   All right.

RICO (*Taking* RUSTY *by the hand*)   Let's go over there, where all of those twinkling white lights are in all of the branches of all of those blinking trees . . .

(They begin to walk together, holding hands, like going steady in high school, maybe)

RUSTY   The Tavern-On-The-Green . . .

RICO   Yeah: that's it. Let's peek in the windows and see how the other half lives. The half that doesn't have to hide. Poor bastards. They don't know what they're missing, by not being the other half: the half that has to hide. No matter what: I wouldn't want it any other way, Rusty. It has so much more meaning this way. Sure, it's harder, but the hardest things in life turn out, in the end, to be the most beautiful things in life . . .

RUSTY   You're so convincing, Rico . . .

(They begin to enter the maze of trees with all of the twinkling lights, and then they begin to peek in the windows of the main dining-room)

RICO   Look at them all!

RUSTY   Shhhhhhh . . . !

RICO   They all look happy, I guess, but none of them could ever be as happy as Rusty and Rico. I mean, baby: we don't need artificial lights in our trees in order to enjoy our dinner, do we now?

RUSTY   Never . . .

RICO *(Looking around)*   I really hate all of these trees being lit up like this. It's not real. You know how I hate anything that has to do with being fake. If I get to be mayor—and *I know* I'll get to be mayor—I'm going to have all of these phoney lights removed from all of these trees. Let the trees grow free and easy, I say. Give the people all a fair chance, I say. But give all of the trees a fair chance, too, I say!

RUSTY   Shhhhhhh . . . !

RICO   Fairness . . . for everybody and everything . . . that's what I believe in.

(RICO *trips on something*)

RUSTY   Be careful, darling . . .

RICO   Well, I'll be . . .

RUSTY   What is it . . .

RICO   I think I know what I tripped on just now.
(RICO *picks up a connected light plug from the ground and shows it to* RUSTY)

RUSTY   It's a light plug . . .

RICO   I'll bet it's the master one . . . I'll bet it connects the whole works. (*Smiling, half-chuckling*) Do you realize what I can do right now, Rusty?

RUSTY   (*Smiling, half-chuckling with him*) I have a funny idea . . .

RICO   Oh, wow . . . !

RUSTY   I dare you . . .
(RICO *grins at* RUSTY *and she grins back, and then he pulls the plug out of the socket. All of the twinkling lights in all of the trees go out at once*)

RICO   Let's get outa here . . . !
(RICO *grabs* RUSTY *by the hand, and then they go scurrying back to the middle of Sheep's Meadow again*)

RUSTY   (*Out of breath*)   Oh, my God . . . what fun that was, Rico!

RICO   You see, Rusty: I got my wish before I even got to be mayor. I guess I'm a pretty lucky guy. Jesus Christ: I feel so special and so powerful: having just done what I just did. What a terrific feeling!

RUSTY   I'm beginning to think that you can do anything you want to do, Rico.
(*They both wink and smile at each other*)

RICO   It's a good life, you know . . . ?

RUSTY   Oh, it's a very good life!

RICO   I wouldn't want it any other way.

RUSTY   I know what you mean.

RICO   I wish that everybody could appreciate life the way that you and I appreciate life.

RUSTY   Well, they could, you know: if they were in love the way that you an I are in love.

RICO   We're really lucky . . . What's wrong?

RUSTY   I'm afraid, Rico.

RICO   Afraid?

RUSTY   Yep.

RICO   Afraid about what?

RUSTY   Afraid about the way that I feel, all of a sudden.

RICO   Geez: I thought you were happy. How do you feel, all of a sudden?

RUSTY   Well, I'll just go right on with it, and I'll tell you: I wanna marry you, Rico. And I wanna have a couple of kids with you, Rico. I wanna settle down.

RICO   Why should that make you afraid?

RUSTY   Because I know that don't want any of that.

RICO   Did I ever say that?

RUSTY   No, but I can just tell.

RICO   Please don't be afraid

RUSTY I'm afraid of something else too, Rico . . .

RICO I said to please don't be afraid, Rusty . . .

RUSTY I'm also afraid of your gun and my gun.

RICO Your gun and my gun?

RUSTY Yes . . .

RICO What are you talking about?

RUSTY You know what I'm talking about!

RICO Now you're getting upset.

RUSTY I am not!

RICO Then why are you yelling all of a sudden like this?

RUSTY Was I yelling?

RICO Real uptight yelling, all of a sudden.

RUSTY Well, I'm sorry: but maybe I have a right to a little uptight yelling.

RICO But why?
(RUSTY *reaches in her handbag and pulls out a small revolver*)

RUSTY This!

RICO I gave you that gun.

RUSTY I know you did. I don't want it anymore.

RICO What do you mean: you don't want it anymore?

RUSTY I don't want to carry it around anymore. I don't like it. I don't like the idea of it. I don't like what it means.

RICO You were okay when I first gave it to you.

RUSTY   Well, I've changed since then.

RICO   But you need it. I gave it to you for protection. You need
something like it in your profession. Just the way I need something like it in my profession too. (*He takes out a small revolver from his coat-pocket*) You see?

RUSTY   I have it!

RICO   But you shouldn't!

RUSTY   It's awful!

RICO   It is not!

RUSTY   I hate it now, Rico! I hate it now because we're fighting.
I don't believe in fighting when you're in love. I especially
don't believe in fighting with the person that you're in love
with. And worse of all: we're fighting over guns: your gun
and my gun! Well, do you love me or don't you love me?!
    (*They both stand there holding their guns in their hands:
    facing each other*)

RICO   Of course I love you, goddammitt!

RUSTY   Then throw it away! Throw your gun away if you love
me! I'm going to throw mine away and so I think it's only right
that you throw yours away too!

RICO   You're freaking out, baby! Is that what you're doing?! Are
you freaking out on me?!

RUSTY   I will freak out if I continue to carry this horrible gun
with me! Just the way I believe that you'll freak out too if you
continue to carry your horrible gun on you!

RICO   Turn some music back on. We need some music right
now.

RUSTY   I'm getting sick.

RICO   I don't want you to get sick.

RUSTY   I'm getting sick because of this horrible gun and because of your horrible gun. I never stop having nightmares every day and every night of the week because I never stop thinking of that horrible gun in your pocket all of the time and this horrible gun in my handbag all of the time. We wear fancy wristwatches which make us feel good because our fancy wristwatches look so good, and they also tell us the time. Well, that's just fine. And we wear precious rings on our fingers, precious rings that you gave to me and that I gave to you simply because you love me and I love you: a green-stoned ring for you and a red-stoned ring for me: red-and-green: stop and go! Green-and-red: go and stop! We make such a marvelous couple, complimenting each other the way that we do. I'm wearing the pink panties with the two bright red hearts made of lovely lace sewed on them that you gave me for Valentine's day. They make me feel so good. And I'm looking at you, and I know that you're wearing the baby-blue boxer shorts made out of pure silk from Italy with two bright red hearts sewn on them which I gave to you for Valentine's Day too. And I can just tell, I can just see it in your beautiful two eyes: that it all makes you feel so good too. I didn't wash my face tonight because you kissed it so much last night, and you didn't shave tonight because I kissed your face so much last night too. (*A pause*) I love you. (*A pause*) I don't know what to do. (*A pause*) I don't know what to with you; I don't know what to do about you. (*A pause*) Because . . . *I love you!* (*A pause*) I'm getting sick to my stomach right now, and my heart and my soul are beginning to ache too: because of this horrible little gun that I carry with me as though it were a wristwatch or a ring or a pair of panties or a face that's not been washed because of your beautiful kiss marks on it. I'm going to throw this horrible little gun away simply because I love you more than anybody else in the whole wide world.

(RUSTY *tosses the revolver away into the darkness*)

RICO   You're crazy, Rusty!

RUSTY   You're the one whose crazy, Rico!

RICO   Listen, I . . .

RUSTY   I don't want to hear! I don't want to hear you say another thing to me until you throw your gun away too?

RICO   Listen, I . . .

RUSTY   Throw it away!

RICO   You're getting hysterical!

RUSTY   Wouldn't you be?!

RICO   For what?!

RUSTY   If you were suddenly sick?!

RICO   I feel all right!

RUSTY   That shocks me!

RICO   Listen, I . . .

RUSTY   It really and truly shocks me!

RICO   Will you please let me finish?!

RUSTY   Okay . . .

RICO   I was going to tell you that I can't throw my "horrible little
         gun" away. I'm a man, and a man can't do something like that.
         Instead of throwing it away I'll just simply put it back in my
         pocket so that you won't be reminded of it, okay?
                  (RICO *places the revolver back in his pocket*)

RICO   There. Okay?
                  (RUSTY *does not answer him*)

RICO   I need to hear some more music now.
                  (RUSTY *stares away from him*)

RICO   Rusty? Did you hear me? Hey, Rusty?! Don't do this to
         me, okay?! I can't take it! I love you! I live you like you're the
         last person on this earth: and that's true, you know? You might
         as well be the last person on this earth because nobody else
         really matters to me. Listen, the reason I can't throw my gun
         away is very obvious and it's also very simple: I can't throw it

away because I'm a man, see? And I'm also a politician, you
know? And a man who is politician as well has just simply got
to behave like a real man: he's got to protect himself and he's
also got to protect the woman that he loves. We live in crazy
times, Rusty: everybody should carry a gun, or a knife, or
something like that. Do you understand what I'm trying to say
to you?

> (RUSTY *turns on the transistor-radio. The music is "This
> Will Be" with Natalie Cole.* RUSTY *begins to dance with
> the music by herself*)

RICO   Jesus, but it's good to see you enjoying yourself again.
Now I can enjoy myself again too.

> (RICO *half-dances around the half-dancing* RUSTY. *He be-
> gins to joke with her as he does a mock version of a
> political speech*)

RICO   Without vitamins these days and these nights we would be
truly lost, beat, hippie, yippie generation, wouldn't we, now?!
We are a vitamin-oriented country, ladies and gentlemen! We
are a nation that is now brought up on vitamin pills! And why
not?!

> (*Sometimes to the audience now, and sometimes to* RUSTY
> *as well*)

RICO   It means we're all very healthy! Right?! RIGHT! Which
means we all vote for the healthiest candidate, the healthiest
man! Without Vitamin A you could not see! Without Vitamin B
you could not keep warm! Without Vitamin C you could not
stop germ invasion! Without Vitamin D you could not develop
in the first place! Without Vitamin E you could not move a
muscle! Without Vitamin F you could not breath or absorb
oxygen! Without Vitamin G you could not think! Without Vitamin K your blood would leak through your blood vessel walls!
Am I telling the truth?!

> (RUSTY *gives in a little bit with a slight smile of approval
> on her face*)

RICO   Then you agree with me?! You have to agree with me!
Without your incomparable Democratic/Liberal candidate running for City Councilman of this district, without him you
could not see, you could not keep warm, you could not stop
germ invasion, you could not develop in the first place, you

could not move a muscle, you could not breath or absorb oxygen, you could not think, and . . .

   (RUSTY *begins to clap her hands in favor of what* RICO *is
   saying*)

RICO   AND . . . ! Your blood would leak through your blood
vessel walls! Without him! And, of course, you all know what
his name is! His name is: RICO ROMA!

   (RUSTY *and* RICO *both applaud together now*)

RICO (*After a nice pause*)   So I guess it's okay again, huh?

RUSTY   What are you talking about?

RICO   I guess we're friends again, right?

RUSTY   I hate to admit it: but I guess so.

RICO   Why do you hate to admit it? You should be happy to
admit it.

RUSTY   Because I'm always giving in to you. Is it because you're
a man and I'm a woman? Or is it because you're such an
appealing turn-on politician? I hope it's because you're the
politician.

RICO (*On an imaginary soapbox*)   Ladies and gentlemen: you
re-elect Rico Roma for City Councilman. Like I said before:
you'll all be helping to keep our district, your district a place
for *people!* Not hamburgers or Medicaid mills!

RUSTY   Now wait just a minute, Mr. Councilman . . . !

RICO   Yes, Miss: I am totally at your disposal. I am your perfect
public servant. What can I do for you, Miss?

RUSTY   I don't like you putting down those hamburger places.
My people would be pretty lost without those hamburgers: the
Jewish people. And what about you're people? The Italians and
the Irish? And what about all of our fellow-people? The Blacks
and the Puerto Ricans and the Poles, and everybody else too?
They really serve a very good purpose: all of those hamburger
places. And those Medicaid mills that you were talking about.

They serve a very good purpose too: for my people, and your people, and all of the people: especially nowadays.

RICO   But I was just simply thinking of the neighborhood that I represent, that's all. I mean if I preached the opposite then I would probably lose the election.

RUSTY   You're always talking about taking a chance, about gambling. So why don't you put your words and your real beliefs into action. And then we'll be able to dance with each other again.

RICO   I'm hip! I'll rewrite the speech within the hour in my head and then I'll say it back to you, and then . . .

RUSTY   And then I want you to write a speech about the whale.

RICO   A speech about the whale?!

RUSTY   They're killing the whale, Rico, they're killing the whale!

RICO   What whale?!

RUSTY   Not just one whale! All of the whales!

RICO   Be more precise, honey.

RUSTY   These men are killing all of these whales. These big business creeps are killing all of the whales simply because of selfish big-pig business. I mean, baby: do you know why they're doing it? Killing that beautiful miraculous creature-creation of that other beautiful miraculous creation: the never-ending ocean, the beautiful bountiful sea! doing it for three things. And do you know what the three things are?! The three things are: *margarine, pet food,* and *shoe polish!* That's what they're killing the wonderful whale for! Can you believe it?! We can all get along without all three of those things, can't we, Rico?

RICO   Of course we can, I guess.

RUSTY   What do you mean: you guess?

RICO   That's what I said: I guess. What's wrong with that? Isn't that what you wanted me to say?

RUSTY   Well, I wanted you to be more positive than that.

RICO   Now you're telling me what to do.

RUSTY   What does that mean?

RICO   It means that now I'm giving in to you: the way you just told me before that you're always giving in to me.

RUSTY   I don't think that's true at all!

RICO   Well, what do you want me to say, for Christ's sake?!

RUSTY   And now we're fighting again, aren't we?!

RICO   I don't think it's a fight. Do you know what the trouble with you is? The trouble with you is that you believe in everything being happy and harmonious and healthy and heartening all of the time. You want everything to be too perfect all of the time.

RUSTY   What's wrong with that? I mean when two people like the two of us are so much in love with each other, well, why shouldn't things be all those things you just told me?!

RICO   Relax!

RUSTY   Maybe you're the one who should relax!

RICO   I'm the most relaxed guy in the world!

RUSTY   Do you really think so?

RICO   I know so! I feel so!

RUSTY   Well, if you're so sure of your state of relaxation . . .

RICO   I'm sure of my state of relaxation all of the time!

RUSTY   Well, if you're so sure of your state of relaxation all of the time: why don't you throw your horrible little gun away?

The way I threw mine away?! That's real proof of being completely relaxed.

RICO   That's what you think. But you're a woman. I suppose a woman is supposed to be that way. Look! Let's stop all of this, okay, Rusty-baby? I mean: I really don't want to disagree with you, I really don't. I'm always trying to keep the love between the two of us a perfect kind of love. Can you buy that? I mean can you buy my sincerity when I say something like that to you?
   (*There is a pause*)

RUSTY   Yes . . . I think I can buy it. I certainly want to buy it.
   (RICO *goes and turns on* RUSTY's *transistor-radio again. This time we hear: O.C. Smith singing: "Could It Be I'm Falling In Love?"* RICO *begins to dance lightly with the music, but* RUSTY *remains rather still*)

RICO   What are you thinking?

RUSTY   Oh, never mind.

RICO   Now you're pouting.

RUSTY   I am not.

RICO   What do you call what you're doing then?

RUSTY   What I'm doing is called: standing. I'm standing in the middle of Sheep's Meadow in Central Park, in the solid heart of the great big red ripe apple, that's what I'm doing. I'm standing here watching my young lover dance for me. When he's not dancing for me he's giving a speech. But I don't mind that because he's supposed to give speeches for everybody else: for the people: his people and my people: all of the people. Because you're in show business. City Councilman. Maybe Mayor somebody. And finally: maybe even President. That's real show business. Everybody thinks they can do a better job than whoever the President is at the time. Oh, why am I going on like this?!
   (RUSTY *switches off the transistor-radio*)

RICO   Now why did you go and do that for?!

RUSTY   This time I'm telling *you* to relax.

RICO   I am relaxed. I was relaxed I'm always relaxed when I'm dancing, and like you said: when I'm giving my speeches for all of the people to hear: my people, your people, all of the people. (*A pause*) Rusty . . . ?

RUSTY   Yes . . . ?

RICO   Who are you? Do you know what I mean, Rusty?

RUSTY   I know what you mean.

RICO   You told me to get rid of my sunglasses, and so, I did: I got rid of my great big expensive sunglasses, didn't I? Because you told me to.

RUSTY   What are you getting at this time?

RICO   I'm getting at the fact that what's fair is fair. Do you know what I'm saying?

RUSTY   I'm not sure yet.

RICO   I got rid of my fake sunglasses because you wanted me to, right?

RUSTY   Right!

RICO   Relax.

RUSTY   I am! For Christ's sake, Rico . . .

RICO   Sorry . . . Well, anyway: I got my rid of my sunglasses, so why don't you get rid of your long golden blonde wig?

RUSTY   Are you serious?

RICO   Yes. I mean: when you really think about it: you really look so much better without it. Shit, baby: you're always talking about male-and-female, lover-and-lover, weddings-and-marriages, ''till death do us part,'' babies-and-families: you're always talking about how it takes ''two-to-tango'' between man-and-woman, how it's a "two-way-street" between husband-and-wife, how it should always be fifty-fifty, no matter how you look at it, right?

RUSTY   Right.

RICO   Well, you see what I'm getting at, Rusty?

RUSTY   Yes, I see.
(RUSTY *slowly removes her long golden blonde wig*)

RUSTY   Okay?

RICO   Terrific!

RUSTY   You really like me this way better?

RICO   There's no other way I could ever like you: but this way! Now throw it away, the way I threw my sunglasses away.
(RUSTY *tosses the long golden blonde wig into the darkness of the night*)

RUSTY   There! Are you happy now?

RICO   Yes. If you're happy too.

RUSTY   I'm always happy if you're happy.

RICO   Then everything is really okay again.

RUSTY   Yes.

RICO (*After a pause*)   I loved being in your bed with you last night.
(RUSTY *smiles at* RICO)

RICO   I love it so much: everytime I come to your place.

RUSTY   What do you mean: *everytime* you come to my place? It's *all* of the time. It would be so nice if I could come to your place once in awhile.

RICO   But you know that's impossible, Rusty!

RUSTY   Yes, I know: but is shouldn't be!

RICO   My career would be ruined if they saw you at my place.

RUSTY   But you don't really know that: I mean: I've never been
to your place. So you really don't know.

RICO   I can't take that chance!
(RUSTY *does not respond*)

RICO   There you go again!

RUSTY   What are you talking about?

RICO   You're pouting again!

RUSTY   I am not!

RICO   What do you call it then?!

RUSTY   It's called quiet silent unspoken thinking. I'm thinking.

RICO   What are you thinking about now?

RUSTY   Now?

RICO   I mean if you're not pouting like you say you're not, then
what are you thinking, like you say you are?

RUSTY   I'm embarrassed to tell you.

RICO   Aw, c'mon . . .

RUSTY   But I am . . .

RICO   But you can't be embarrassed because it's me you're deal-
ing with. Remember me?

RUSTY   Oh, Rico, how could I ever forget you?

RICO   So what are you embarrassed to tell me?

RUSTY   Let's smoke a joint first. And then I'll tell you, okay?

RICO   Okay.
        (RUSTY *takes a joint out of her handbag. She lights it,
        sucks in, and then hands it to* RICO)

RUSTY   Oh, Rico.

RICO   Oh, Rusty.
        (RUSTY *receives the joint back from* RICO)

RUSTY   Oh, my sweet Rico.

RICO   Oh, my double-sweet Rusty. Tell me what you're embar-
        rassed to tell me.

RUSTY   (*After a pause*)   I'm embarrassed to tell you . . . that
        the two of us . . . are beginning to remind me of . . .
        Romeo and Juliet!

RICO   Romeo and Juliet?!

RUSTY   I can't go to your place, you can only go to my place. We
        always have to meet in secret on the streets and in deserted
        street corners. Or we have to take a cheap hotel room some-
        where in Times Square. Or we have to drive to the suburbs and
        park secretly on the side of some deserted road and then climb
        into the back seat together. I mean, Rico, it's awfully crowded
        in the back seat of your car, even though . . .

RICO   Even though that was the best time we ever fucked!

RUSTY   I was just going to say the same thing.

RICO   But why are you embarrassed about being like Romeo and
        Juliet?

RUSTY   Because, maybe: it's too romantic to even think about,
        that's why. And it's also scaring me.

RICO   Scaring you?

RUSTY   Yes.

RICO   But why?

RUSTY Well, it ends up tragically, doesn't it? Romeo and Juliet? That's what scares me.

RICO Forget it.

RUSTY I just wish our didn't give the impression of being a forbidden love, that's all I'm really saying, Rico.

RICO But don't you think it's really sort of exciting that way? Don't you almost think that it's even more of a turn-on this way?

RUSTY I don't know. Maybe you're right.
(*Suddenly we hear a strange sound in the distance. It is rather foreboding*)

RICO Did you hear that?!
(RICO *pulls out his tiny revolver*)

RUSTY Yes.

RICO What was it?! Whose there?!
(RICO *begins to look about the area, forever waving his tiny revolver*)

RUSTY Please put it away!

RICO Where are you?!

RUSTY Please put it away!

RICO Come out: wherever you are!

RUSTY Oh, Rico!

RICO Will you lay off, Rusty?!

RUSTY I want you to put that gun away! I want you to throw that horrible little gun away!

RICO No way! We're in trouble, I think.

RUSTY   We are not!

RICO   You heard that noise, didn't you?!

RUSTY   It could have been anything!

RICO   It was a really strange noise! I don't trust it! The sound of
it: it makes me suspiscious!

RICO   It could have been anything.
(RICO *paces back-and-forth with his tiny revolver; it is as
though he is acting out a scene from a murder-mystery
movie*)

RICO   We can't take that chance!

RUSTY   We only heard it once. It was nothing. It could have been
anything. There are eight million people living here. And so,
what's the big deal about a strange noise all of a sudden? Well,
maybe I've got the answer to that one, Rico! You know what
the big deal is?! The big deal is that when you carry a gun on
you all of the time, well, eventually, no matter what, you just
gotta find a way to use it, no matter what! And that's what
you're doing right now! And I think it's awful, Rico, I really
do!
(RICO *calms down a little bit*)

RICO   You're nuts, Rusty-baby! I'm trying to protect you! That's
what a man's supposed to do, goddammitt, so don't be trying to
cut off my balls, okay?!

RUSTY   What did you say?!

RICO   You heard me! You just let me be a man when I'm supposed to be a man and I'll let you be a woman when you're
supposed to be a woman. (RICO *slows down now*) And when I
put this gun away it's because I wanted to put it away, it's
because I felt it was okay to put it away, and it had nothing to
do with you wanting me to put it away.
(RICO *puts his gun away*)

RUSTY   (*After a pause*)   Why don't you try screwing with it?!
Why don't you try fucking with it?!

RICO   What the fuck's going on with you?! Listen . . . I'm
trying to be calm . . . and I'm trying to relax . . . and I'm
really trying to understand where you're head is coming at. I'm
a politician, remember? And a politician has to be patient,
remember? I'm really being extra-patient with you right now,
Rusty. (*A pause*) And do you know why? Well, the reason why
is simple . . . the is because—no matter what you might
think sometimes—the reason for my extra-patience with you is
simply because I love you. I love you so much, baby, I love
you so gaddam much that I want to eat you up and I don't ever
want to digest you once I've eaten you! That's how much I love
you!

(RUSTY *says nothing; she is rather moved all of a sudden*)

RICO   Okay . . . ?
(*Silence*)

RICO (*Smiling*)   So what can I do for you, Miss? I mean once
you've voted for me and re-elected me: what can I do for you?

RUSTY (*Half-smiling*)   You can write that speech about the
whale. And you can give that speech about the whale.

RICO   It's a deal. Now tell me again: what are they killing all of
the whales for?

RUSTY   They're killing all of the whales for three things: for
margarine, for *pet food,* and for *shoe polish.*

RICO   Well, I never use margarine, pet food, and shoe polish.

RUSTY   And that's the whole point, Mr. Councilman. My God,
sir: margarine costs more nowadays than pure rich creamery
butter. And there is a difference, honey, between butter and
margarine!

RICO   And pet food?!

RUSTY   Well, if you really and truly love your pets—dogs, cats,
birds, goldfish, whatever—well, you should feed them the
same food that you eat, don't you think, Rico?

RICO   It sounds ethical to me.

RUSTY   And shoe polish . . .

RICO   Yeah, what about shoe polish?

RUSTY   Well, shoe polish is just plain downright ridiculous! Shoes don't really need to shine. Shoes should be raunchy-looking, they need to be well-broken-in and extremely comfortable, don't you think, Rico?

RICO   That's exactly what I think, Rusty.

RUSTY   You're changing, Rico.

RICO   Changing?

RUSTY   Yes.

RICO   Changing for the better?

RUSTY   Oh, of course: for the better.

RICO   Okay . . .

RUSTY   Oh, it's really okay . . .

RICO   Right on . . .

RUSTY   Right on . . . forever . . .
          (*There is a loving pause between the two of them now*)

RUSTY (*Finally*)   Rico . . . ?

RICO   What's up, baby?

RUSTY   I need a few more puffs.

RICO   I know what you mean.

RUSTY   Life can be so wonderful, *sometimes,* that's why I need a few more puffs.

RICO   I know what you mean.
          (*This time* RICO *takes out a joint. He lights it, sucks in, and then hands it to* RUSTY. *She sucks in a few times also*)

RICO   Nice stuff, huh?

RUSTY   Real nice. Better than my stuff, huh?

RICO   I wouldn't say that. I think you're stuff is your thing and my stuff is my thing. I think we both got good fine grass going for us.

RUSTY   You're being a gentleman now.

RICO   That's because I'm with this lady-of-all-ladies right now.

RUSTY   You're such a sweet candy bar.

RICO   Bite me then.
        (RUSTY *gives him a harmless bite on the face*)

RUSTY   Okay?

RICO   Okay. But now it's my turn.
        (RICO *gives her a harmless bite where her crotch is*)

RUSTY   You naughty boy, Rico.

RICO   I love it.
        (RUSTY *looks far off into the distance*)

RUSTY   Do you know what I would like to do? I would like to take an elevator up to the top of the Waldorf-Astoria Towers.
        (RICO *looks far off into the distance too*)

RICO   And then what would you do?

RUSTY   I would pass this juicy joyful joint of such green and gorgeous extra-good grass, I would pass it around from suite-to-suite of the Waldorf-Astoria Towers: offering it to The Shah of Iran, The Queen of the Netherlands, that Princess from England, to Cassius Clay Himself, to Richard M. Nixon incognito—he really deserves to be free and relax—the soft part of my heart tells—and even to Mamie Eisenhower, although from what I've heard: she's always been free and relaxed.

RICO   Right on, Mamie!

(RUSTY *and* RICO *finish the joint together. Then she turns the transistor-radio back on again: The Bee Gee's are singing "Jive Talkin'"*)

RICO   You know something, Rusty?

RUSTY   Yes, sweetheart?

RICO   I really don't want to change. I really want to grow. And I really don't want you to change, either: I really want you to grow.

RUSTY   It sounds terrific, Rico.

RICO   What's your favorite flower?

RUSTY (*After a pause*)   The gardenia.

RICO   Good. The gardenia. And so: let's pretend that *you're* a gardenia. Instead of changing—because you don't want it to change, I don't want it to change, I want it to stay just like it is, I want you to stay just like you are—instead of changing: the gardenia *grows!* It gets bigger and bigger. It's smooth ivory petals, so soft and sweet and delicate, well, they become larger and larger. Its deep forest green leaves, glistening so nicely in the moonlight: they become fuller and fuller. And then there's the stem: the exciting stem of the exotic erotic gardenia becomes richer and richer and taller and taller. And, finally: there is its fantastic smell: the lovely luscious odor and scent of the gardenia becomes even more fantastic than it ever was before. It never stops growing: it goes on forever and ever! And while it grows, well, while it matures and spreads out and grows without ever once stopping, while it does all of this—the whole complete plant of the gardenia—while it does all of this: it also never changes! No way does it ever change! And that's what it's all about, my beautiful little-big Rusty-baby-honey. Forever . . .

RUSTY   . . . and ever!
        (RUSTY *kisses* RICO *on the lips*)

RICO   You see?

RUSTY   See what?

RICO   That kiss you just gave to me . . . ?

RUSTY   Yes . . . ?

RICO   Well, it's never going to change: it's just going to stay with me *forever,* that's all.

RUSTY   What about you?

RICO   What about me?

RUSTY   If you give me a kiss now: will it be the same way?

RICO   Shall I try?

RUSTY   Yes.

RICO   And then we'll see what happens, okay?

RUSTY   Okay.
(RICO *kisses* RUSTY *on the lips*)

RUSTY   You see?

RICO   See what?

RUSTY   That kiss you just gave to me . . . ?

RICO   Yes . . . ?

RUSTY   Well, it's never going to change, either: it's just going to stay with me *forever,* too, that's all.
(RUSTY *and* RICO *stand there in the meadow—just simply facing each other now: smiling and silent. But eventually the silence is broken by fire engines in the distance; the sirens of the fire engines become louder and louder; the smiles on the faces of* RUSTY *and* RICO *fade a little bit; the fire engine sirens go away into the night; the smiles on the faces of* RUSTY *and* RICO *come back to fullness again*)

RICO (*Finally*)   What are you thinking now?

RUSTY   Ah, Rico, Rico, where for art thou, Rico!

RICO I'm right here, Rusty, *forever!*

RUSTY My love for you, Rico, well, it ain't *changing,* no way, sweet candy-bar.

RICO What's it doin' then, baby?

RUSTY *It's growing!*
(*Suddenly there is a loud thunderous sound of crashing glass coming from somewhere.* RICO *immediately pulls out his tiny revolver*)

RICO Who is it?! Whose there?! Don't move! I got you covered! Whoever you are! You don't have a chance! You understand?! Where are you?!

RUSTY Oh, Rico . . . !

RICO Shhhhhhh! He'll hear you! They'll hear you!

RUSTY Oh, please, Rico, please . . . !

RICO SHHHHHHH!
(RICO *begins to stalk the whole area, back-and-forth, with his waving little revolver*)

RUSTY But it was only some glass crashing, that's all . . .

RICO I told you to be quiet!

RUSTY But you're acting so foolish, Rico . . .

RICO Come out, wherever you are! Whoever you are! Come out right now! Otherwise you're dead!
(RUSTY *begins to move away from* RICO)

RUSTY I'm going . . .

RICO What?!

RUSTY I said I'm going . . .

RICO Don't go!

RUSTY   Only if you put away that horrible little gun.

RICO   That would be suicide! For the both of us!

RUSTY   I don't even want you to put that horrible little gun away.
I want you to *throw* it away! For good! *Forever and ever!*
        (RICO *continues to "stalk" his "enemy"*)

RICO   Stay with me, Rusty, please?! You stay with me and
everything will be okay! OKAY?!

RUSTY   But I can't . . .

RICO   Why are you being so stubborn?!

RUSTY   Why are *you* being so stubborn?!
        (*We hear the soft barking of a dog in the distance.* RICO
        reacts to it almost violently)

RICO (*Waving his tiny revolver*)   Who is it?! WHO IS IT?!

RUSTY (*Desperately*)   It's only a dog!
        (RICO *begins to head in the direction of the barking dog*)

RICO   Come on out! C'MON!

RUSTY   It's a dog I said!

RICO   C'MON OUT WITH YOUR HANDS UP! C'MON NOW!
        (RICO *goes in-and-out of the dark shadows while he waves
        his tiny revolver madly before him in the air*)

RUSTY   Will you please listen to me, Rico?!
        (*We hear the barking of the dog coming closer;* RICO *is on
        the verge of panic almost*)

RICO   He's getting closer!

RUSTY   I can't stand this!
        (*The dog is barking louder now*)

RICO   *They're* getting closer!

RUSTY   I'm going to stop you, Rico!
(RUSTY *begins to move towards* RICO. *The barking of the dog is almost on top of them now.* RICO *begins to aim at the darkness and the area where the barking of the dog is coming from*)

RICO   You're not going to get me! You're not going to get her! We're like Romeo and Juliet! We're even better than Romeo and Juliet!

RUSTY   Stop it, Rico, stop it!
(RICO *is just about ready to pull the trigger of his tiny revolver which is aimed directly at the sound of the barking dog in the distant darkness; but* RUSTY *comes fast upon him; she pushes* RICO's *arm fast up into the air so that when he pulls the trigger the shots go upward instead of the direction in which he was aiming; the dog's barking is loud and hysterical now*)

RICO (*To* RUSTY)   You're freaking out, baby!

RUSTY   No, not me! YOU!
(RUSTY *and* RICO *begin to struggle: she is trying to get the gun from out of his hand. We hear the dog go barking off in the distance*)

RICO (*Struggling to keep the gun in his hand*)   What kind of Juliet are you, anyway?!

RUSTY (*Losing the battle*)   What sort of a Romeo . . . ARE YOU?!
(*They both continue to struggle; it is obvious that* RUSTY *has more strength than one would have believed. Suddenly we hear a whole pack of dogs approaching in the distance: all sorts of various barking and howling: growing louder and louder. For the moment:* RUSTY *and* RICO *freeze in their physical struggle*)

RICO   Oh, my God! Listen to them! There's more than one this time! A wild pack of wild dogs, getting closer, hungrier! They're going to get us, Juliet, if we don't get them first! LISTEN TO THEM!
(*The barking and howling of all of the dogs grows to an*

extreme pitch. RICO *begins to wave his gun again: in all sorts of wild directions*)

RUSTY   Oh, Romeo, Rico: I don't hear anything! What's wrong with you, Rico?! Please . . . ?!
(*The barking and howling of all of the dogs disappears almost instantly. But* RICO *continues to wave the gun wildly in the air, and so,* RUSTY *begins to struggle with him again. Eventually, the tiny revolver is dragged down to the waist area of* RICO)

RICO   You've gone crazy!

RUSTY   You *are* crazy!
(RUSTY *almost gets the tiny revolver out of* RICO's *hand, but as they both struggle with it,* RICO *accidentally pulls the trigger. We hear the shot ring out.* RUSTY *lets out a devastating cry.* RICO *has been shot by himself in the stomach. The tiny revolver drops out of his hand and falls to the ground.* RICO *begins to fall while* RUSTY *hangs onto him for dear life. Finally, they both fall down together,* RUSTY *cradling* RICO *in her arms while he lies down on his back. Very far off in the distance we can hear the barking of the first lone dog, and then, it finally is gone*)

RUSTY   Oh, my sweet candy-bar, Rico . . .

RICO   I didn't hurt the dog . . . did I . . . the first little dog that we heard . . . ?

RUSTY   No, no. the first little dog's okay.

RICO   I'm glad . . . of that . . .
(RUSTY's *eyes are beginning to tear*)

RUSTY   Please be still. Don't talk. Don't do anything. I'll get you to a hospital. The doctors will help you. The nurses will take care of you. I'll be with you all of the time. Oh, Rico, why did this have to happen?!

RICO   I'd much rather have a priest around, instead of doctors and nurses. I'd much rather have *you* around . . . instead of anybody else. (*A pause*) I ain't feelin' too good, Rusty. (*A *pause*) One thing, one thing I gotta tell you: if I split, and I really think I'm splitting . . . if I split right here . . . before you can do anything for me . . . and I got this real bad vibration that nobody can do anything for me now . . .

RUSTY   Please don't talk . . . Rico . . .

RICO   If I split, well, I just want you to remember what I told you about the gardenia, that's all. The gardenia lives on *forever!* And *you're* the gardenia . . . remember? And remember this too: I'd like a few flowers on my coffin when they finally lower it into my grave . . . and do you know why? Because I don't think I told you: but the gardenia is my favorite flower too. And so, do you know what that means, Rusty? It means that were both gardenias: always growing, but never changing, always growing forever and ever!

(RICO *dies in* RUSTY's *arm. She does not sob however, even though her eyes are full of quiet tears now. She stares into his face for a very long time. Then she takes the tiny revolver from out of his lifeless hand. She looks at it in her own hand now. At first she is very cautious with it; eventually she is very reckless with it. She presses the nozzle of it into her stomach. She closes her eyes and pulls the trigger. Nothing happens. She pulls the trigger again. Nothing happens. And again. And nothing happens. She becomes hysterical and impatient. She continues to pull the trigger. It is obvious the gun is empty of bullets. She begins to laugh softly, half-mockingly. She looks into* RICO's *face*)

RUSTY   Can you believe it? I don't believe it. But Rico: what about my horrible little gun? The one that you gave to me? The one that I threw away tonight? Remember? It must be around somewhere, don't you think so, Rico? I won't be gone long. Just for a moment or two, until I find it, that's all. And then I'll come back to you, that's all.

(RUSTY *kisses* RICO *on his dead lips. Slowly she gets up. She moves away from him and eventually she disappears into the darkness. There is a pause. And then we hear one single gun shot ring out in the air. Another pause. And dead silence. Presently,* RUSTY *appears in the area again. She is clutching at her stomach. She half-walks to* RICO's *body, and then, very slowly, she falls down in a kneeling position beside him. She looks into his face once again*)

RUSTY   How about some music, sweet candy-bar? So that we can dance again?

> (RUSTY *reaches over and turns on her transistor-radio. The music is the same music that we heard at the beginning of the play: "The Love I Lost" sung by Harold Melvin and the Blue Notes*)

RUSTY (*To* RICO's *dead face*)   My love for you ain't changing, Rico. It's *growing*, baby!

> (RUSTY *falls over* RUSTY's *body very gently, cradling him again, and then she also dies. The lights begin to dim very slowly. We hear an emergency police siren going on-and-off in the far distance, and we also are aware of the flashing spotlight in the distance coming from atop the emergency police car. And then we hear static coming from the transistor-radio. The music is interrupted*)

RADIO ANNOUNCER   This is station WRRS. We are sorry to interrupt this program, but for those of you who stayed tuned in during all these wee hours of the morning, here in New York Town, we thought that it might be appropriate at this time to bring you rather sad and rather tragic news. Just a little while ago, over in Central Park, right smack in the middle of Sheep's Meadow, two lovers were found dead in each other's arms. The identity of the man and the woman is being held confidential until their next of kin are notified . . .

> (*The* VOICE *of the* RADIO ANNOUNCER *is now drowned out by the approaching sounds of the emergency sirens coming from the emergency police cars. There is a wild flashing of police emergency lights as the lights continue to dim out on the bodies of* RUSTY *and* RICO)

Blackness

Lena and Louie

THE PEOPLE OF THE PLAY
(as they appear)

LENA: A terrific-looking Italian-American woman, youngish, who also possesses a terrific-looking body and who is a lady-hobo who lives and loves all over the streets and the avenues of New York City.

LOUIE: a handsome macho-looking guy with lots of enticing energy and a gleaming head of sandy-colored hair who is maybe a little younger than LENA and who is part Polish, part Jewish, part Puerto Rican, and part Black, and who is a gentleman-hobo and who lives and loves all over the streets and the avenues of New York City.

WHERE THEY ARE

LENA and LOUIE: all over ''The Big Apple,'' and, in the end: in Central Park.

WHEN

LENA and LOUIE: anytime afterwards.

Lena and Louie

The stage area is in complete darkness: as we left it at the end of the first act. In the pitch blackness of the stage and the theater we hear the VOICE *of a* WOMAN RADIO ANNOUNCER *this time: coming over another transistor-radio.*

RADIO ANNOUNCER   The identifications of the two dead bodies of the handsome young man and the beautiful older woman that were found together in each other's arms in the middle of Sheep's Meadow in Central Park around midnight last night have now been made known to the public . . .

(The lights begin to come up very slowly on the stage area)

RADIO ANNOUNCER   The handsome young dead man has been identified as Rico Roma, the semi-known City Councilman who was in the process of trying to be re-elected again . . .

(As the lights onstage continue to come up very slowly we notice LENA: *she comes onstage pushing a beat-up grocery-store cart that is filled with all of her wordly possessions. She holds her transistor-radio to her left ear)*

RADIO ANNOUNCER   The beautiful young dead woman has been identified as Rebecca "Rusty" Rubinstein, who was an unknown nighttime woman of the midtown East Side Streets . . .

(The lights are almost all the way up now. LENA *looks up at the sky: it is still dark outside, although it is approaching dawn)*

RADIO ANNOUNCER   The detectives of Manhattan and the doctors of Manhattan have all agreed to the dramatic and theatrical fact that it appears to have been a love-pact dual-suicide . . .

(The lights are all the way up now. LENA *goes through her cart until she finds a plastic kerchief for her head. She puts it on. It is obviously raining now. She takes a book from out of a paper bag. She sits down and begins to read the book in the rain. You would think that she was cozily at home in front of a wood-burning fireplace. Eventually, a bright sign comes into view in the distance. It says: THE NEW YORK EXPERIENCE! 2nd SMASH YEAR!)*

(*And now:* LOUIE *enters. He carries a transistor-radio
also, and he also pushes a beat-up grocery-store cart. He
gives* LENA *a knowing glance and then she returns it, and
then she goes back to reading her book.* LOUIE *pulls an
umbrella from out of his grocery-cart. He opens it up. It's
full of holes and most of the spokes are broken*)

LENA (*Reading her book*)   Forget it.

LOUIE   It used to be okay: when it was new.

LENA (*Reading her book*)   You never had anything that was new.

LOUIE   That's not true, Lena.

LENA (*Reading from her book*)   Stop kidding yourself, Louie.
Just be yourself, Pussycat.

LOUIE (*Sitting opposite* LENA)   Okay.
(*Another bright sign comes on in the distance. It says:*
McGRAW-HILL)

LENA (*Reading from her book*)   The rain feels good, Louie.
Especially tonight: it feels good)
(LOUIE *closes the useless umbrella; he places it back in his*
grocery-store cart)

LOUIE   The night's almost over with. It's gonna be daylight
soon. It's gonna be a beautiful new dawn before we even know
it. Hey, Lena: you know something? You'll never change.

LENA (*Reading from her book*)   What are you implying, Louie?

LOUIE   I'm not implying anything: I'm telling you. You'll never
change. And I mean it in a very positive way. Who else reads
outside when it's raining? Only you. Lena. *My* Lena. And
that's why I love you.

LENA (*Reading from her book*)   You proposing again?

LOUIE   Maybe.

LENA (*Reading from her book*)   Just let me finish this last speech
of Ophelia's, okay, Louie?

LOUIE   Okay.

LENA   And then I'll be able to talk to you without any distractions.

LOUIE   Right on.
(LENA *finishes reading. She closes the book, after wiping the raindrops from it*)

LOUIE   What are you doing?

LENA   I'm wiping the raindrops off the pages of my book.
(LENA *places the book carefully back into her cart*)

LOUIE   It's almost as though you were wiping teardrops instead of raindrops.

LENA   Maybe it looked that way to you because I just finished reading Ophelia's last speech.

LOUIE   I guess that's it then.

LENA (*Making herself comfortable*)   Okay now, Louie.

LOUIE   Okay now what, Lena?

LENA   Okay now: I'm ready to talk to you without being distracted.

LOUIE   Oh, good. Who were you reading?

LENA   William Shakespeare, of course.

LOUIE   I'm very impressed. I wish he was alive. Today. Right now. Then he'd really have something to write about.

LENA   He did pretty good even then.

LOUIE   What are you doing here tonight, by the way, if you don't mind my asking?

LENA   I like the fountains and the silver reflections, by the way, if you don't mind my telling you.

LOUIE   I don't mind.

LENA   I made five dollars today.

LOUIE   Honest?!

LENA   Well, a lot of it has to do with the fact that I prayed a whole lot last night. I prayed last night more than I think I've ever prayed before in my whole life.

LOUIE   Where were you last night?

LENA   I slept right behind St. Patrick's Cathedral last night. Never did that trip before. I guess that's why I automatically prayed more than I ever did before: last night. The surrounding atmosphere, Louie, ya' dig? The church, the spires of the church: me relaxing in the shadows of the church and the spires of the church. I got a little sad too. I thought of Bobby Kennedy's funeral. Remember, Louie?
(LOUIE *nods his head sadly*)

LOUIE   I remember . . .

LENA   I thought of other funerals too: but it really Bobby's that stuck in my mind the whole night last night. Well, anyway: it really paid off last night, didn't it? My praying my ass off the way that I did, last night.

LOUIE   It sure did. Five dollars! I only came up with seventy-five cents today, Lena.

LENA   Where did you sleep last night?

LOUIE   Near the U.N.

LENA   No wonder you only ended up with seventy-five cents.

LOUIE   But I'm richer for it in another way. I met a bunch of Hungarians, a bunch of Russians, a bunch of Irish, a bunch of Italians, a bunch of Jews, a bunch of Blacks, a bunch of English, a bunch of Germans, a bunch of Polish, a bunch of Chinese, a bunch of Japanese, a bunch of Koreans, a bunch of Puerto Ricans, a bunch of Protestansts, a bunch of Spanish, a bunch of Scandinavians, a bunch of Australians, a bunch of. . .

    (LENA *takes off her plastic rainproof kerchief and places it back somewhere carefully in her grocery-store cart*)

LOUIE   . . . taxicab drivers, a bunch of prostitutes, a bunch of people on welfare, a bunch of people with V.D., a bunch of rich people who were drunk and falling out of their limousines, and a bunch of people who just finally didn't give a good fuck anymore because that's what they thought they were supposed to think nowadays.

LENA   Some night for you, Louie.

LOUIE   Yeah, it sure was. I felt right at home: I mean I got to thinking about what I am, if you know what I mean? I thought about my blood, my rainbow-colored blood that's always going through my whole rainbow-colored system. I thought about being part Irish, part Jewish, part Puerto Rican, and part Black. That's why I really felt at home last night: even if I only came up with seventy-five cents for the day.

LENA   You're making me jealous?

LOUIE   How come?

LENA   Well, all I got is all Italian blood in me. I feel like maybe I've been gyped. I don't feel like a rainbow, the way that you feel like a rainbow, Louie.

LOUIE   Don't let it bother you, Lena. I like you just the way you are: with all of that Italian blood. Remember that time when you cut your finger in front of George Washington's statue down on Wall Street?

LENA   I'll never forget it. It gives me the chills just to think about it. Look at the scar yet.

    (LENA *extends her scarred finger to* LOUIE; *he kisses it*)

LOUIE   You were trying to be too European that night. You were cutting up that big fat juicy orange. But remember what I did?

LENA   Oh, that was beautiful: what you did! I'll never forget it for as long as I live.

LOUIE   You were really bleeding, blood all over the steps of that building, Federal Hall, where George Washington made his first speech to our country as the first president of our country.

LENA   You knew I was an acute bleeder and so you just took my bleeding gushing finger into your mouth and you drank the blood and sucked on my finger until the bleeding finally stopped. I couldn't believe it.

LOUIE   Well, if you weren't an Italian-American, Lena, I don't know whether I would have done that or not. All I do know is that blood of yours reminded me of red Italian wine. It was like a combination of Bardolino and Valpolicella, and I just know that it had to do with you being Italian, so don't feel like you been gyped, okay, Lena?

LENA   Okay.

LOUIE   Listen, no matter what, last night near the U.N. Building, even though all of those bunches of people were there too, no matter what: I always thought of you first, and I always was thinking of you the whole time too.

LENA   You're really such a pussycat. I love you.

LOUIE   The feeling's mutual, believe me: when I tell you that.

LENA   I do, I do.
        (*There is a pause. They both look rather lovingly at each other*)

LOUIE   What are you going to do with the five dollars?

LENA   I knew you'd be asking me that. Well, first of all I've decided to split it with you.

LOUIE   Aw, you don't have to.

LENA   But I want to. Now first of all, we're not taking any subways, no buses, nothing, since that goddam stupid fare went up to fifty cents. I'll tell you something, Pussycat Louie: we're not even going to take the Staten Island Ferry anymore since it went up to a quarter . . .

LOUIE   But it's for a round trip . . .

LENA   I don't care! Not at this stage of the game anyway: I don't care! Now what we're both going to do this: we're going to go shopping tomorrow. We're going to spend all of my money on things to eat . . . and drink. You know I can't eat without wine with every meal. Oh, by the way: what about your friend who works at Maxwell's Plum? He didn't quit yet, did he?

LOUIE   He got fired instead.

LENA   Oh, that's terrible . . . !

LOUIE   But it's okay, believe me, Lena. I got this other friend who works at *Lutece*.

LENA   You're kidding?! *Lutece?!*

LOUIE   That's right: *Lutece!* And he told me he'd keep me sup-plied, and in turn, I'd be keeping you supplied, just like al-ways, Lena. Look . . .
(LOUIE *takes a bottle of red wine from out of his shopping cart. It's been opened and only about a half-glass has been taken from it, and now it's re-corked*)

LENA   Oh, dynamite, Louie Pussycat!

LOUIE   Some couple from Florida only tried it out but then they kept right on drinking their Miller's High Life and vodka sting-ers while they ate their dinner.

LENA   They did this at *Lutece?!*

LOUIE   That's right . . .

LENA   Oh, dear . . .

LOUIE   And so my friend thought of me immediately. I went by and picked it up this afternoon from one of the assistant chefs.

LENA   What's the name of it?

LOUIE   Well, you know the reputations of Americans in interna-
tional wine circles: they're name buyers. They almost always
go straight for the Chateau Lafite-Rothschild; or in other va-
rieties, well, straight for the Dom Perignon, the Chateau-neuf-
du-Pape, the Pommard, Pouilly-Fuisse, or the California
cabernet sauvignon . . .
    (*He pronounces them all incorrectly, but* LENA *knows
what he's talking about*)

LOUIE   Well, baby . . . It's the Chateau Lafite-Rothschild!

LENA   Oh, I feel so good already! We'll go shopping just as soon
as daylight comes. Let's go down to that A-&-P in The Village
that stays open until midnight and that opens up very early in
the morning. We'll walk. It'll be good for us. After all: we'll
have something to look forward to, won't we, Louie? We'll go
down there and buy lots of cheeses, or at least a little bit of
cheese, since the price of cheese these days is just simply
outrageous, and we'll buy some fruit, apples and peaches
mostly, and some bread, or maybe crackers instead if they got
one of those markdowns like they usually have on those elegant
foreign crackers from France or someplace like that, and a fresh
dill pickle for you and a fresh dill pickle for me, and oh, yes, a
nice hunk of A-&-P liverwurst which we can make-believe is-
some fancy French pate with truffles which we'll wash down
with our elegant exotic excellent extremly expert-type of delicious red wine. It'll be a nice day, today, won't it, Pussycat
Louie?
    (LOUIE *nods happily like a happy little boy*)

LENA   I love you, Louie. Do you think that when tonight comes
again we can find a new place where we can spend the whole
night together without the cops bothering us? I love you, Louie.

LOUIE   I love you too, Lena.

LENA   By the way, I do know of a new place. That little plaza
behind the Burlington Mills Building between the Ziegfeld
Theatre. It's got those fountains too that they don't turn off.
It'll be so nice and so romantic to have you fuck me to the
rippling watery sounds of those rippling watery fountains . . .

LOUIE   To have me *make love* to you, Lena . . .

LENA   Okay then: it'll be so nice to have you *make love* to me. Oh, my Louie! My rainbow-colored Louie from The Bronx! You're such a rainbow-blooded mixed-up breed-of-a-man when it comes to *balling!*

LOUIE   And you, Lena, oh, Lena! From the heart of Little Italy! You're such an Italian lady when it comes to *making love!*

LENA   Who would you like to be tonight, Louie?

LOUIE   Who would you like me to be?

LENA   I'd like you to be *John Lindsay* tonight.

LOUIE   That's going to be hard, Lena. We don't look nothing alike.

LENA   But you can do it. You can do anything, Louie.

LOUIE   Okay then: I'll be John Lindsay tonight. But you know . . . ?

LENA   Yes, Pussycat Louie . . . ?

LOUIE   Well, you sure you don't want me to be Joe Namath again? It was really so easy for me to be Willy-Joe.

LENA   We'll do that trip another time.

LOUIE   Remember who you were on that rip, Lena?

LENA   I loved it! I was Gloria Steinem!
         (*There is another pause: They both look lovingly at each other again*)

LOUIE   I love you, Lena.

LENA   And I love you too, Louie.

LOUIE   Well, since you want me to be John Lindsay tonight after we have our dinner together: do you know who I want you to be?

LENA   I'm waiting.

LOUIE   I want you to be *Jackie!*

LENA   Oh, I'd love that, Pussycat Louie! *John and Jackie!*
Jackie and John! That's a real trip, Louie, don't you think?

LOUIE   Not bad at all!

LENA   Me?! Lena Marie Gusto from the heart of Little Italy
being Jacqueline Bouvier Kennedy Onassis making love with
our former Mayor John V. Lindsay! What a terrific trip, Louie!

LOUIE   I can hardly wait, Lena.
        (*There is another pause*)

LENA   I love you, Louie.

LOUIE   I love you too, Lena.

LENA   We're really lucky . . .

LOUIE   I know . . .

LENA   Tonight is going to be such a terrific trip for the two of us.
Such a tempting tempetuous torrid tropical night right here in the
middle of the heart of the big red juicy bright shining apple.
And then the real time arrives: the real nighttime arrives, and it
takes us to the quiet and peaceful area of Burlington Mills and
Ziegfeld with those tiny little fountains playing soft splashing
water sounds for us: a free and flowing water symphony, just
like in Rome, while we become John V. Lindsay and
Jacqueline Bouvier Kennedy Onassis: and we fuck—I mean
ball!—I'm sorry, Pussycat Louie: I mean: *make love:* we make
love for the rest of the nocturnal big city night in nice ole' New
York Town: lonely town and *only* town. I love you,
Louie . . .

LOUIE   I love you too, Lena . . .

LENA   Louie . . . ?

LOUIE   I'm here, Lena . . .

LENA   How are you doing?

LOUIE   How are *you* doing?

LENA   I asked you first, Pussycat Louie.

LOUIE   I'm doing okay as long as you're doing okay. Are you doing okay, Lena?

LENA   I'm doing really okay.

LOUIE   Me too: Lena Marie Gusto from the heart of Little Italy.

LENA   Right on: Louie Rainbow from the heart of The Golden Melting Pot.
        (*They both look into each other's eyes. By now the dark-ness has disappeared. It is dawn, and the sun is coming up*)

LOUIE   It's the beginning of a new day.

LENA   I wonder what the new day has in store for us.

LOUIE   Let's not even think about it. If we think about it, well, it might not be such a good day in the end.

LENA   I know what you mean.

LOUIE   I was just thinking: remember that time in front of The Frick?

LENA   How could I forget it?

LOUIE   That was the best time that we ever made love, re-member?

LENA   It really was the best time. But do you know what I'm thinking now? Do you know what I think is going to happen today? Or better still: tonight? I think tonight is going to be the best night that we ever made love, I really do, Louie.

LOUIE   How come?

LENA   I don't know. I can't really explain it. I can only just feel it.

LOUIE   You mean like you can just feel it in the air?

LENA   Yes, I can just feel it in the air: it's the vibrations that I'm feeling: in the air.

LOUIE   You really got me convinced.

LENA   You're not putting me on now, are you?

LOUIE   Oh, no: I'm really convinced.

LOUIE   I mean I can just see it in your eyes. I can just tell by the sound in your voice. I'm noticing it in the way that your whole body is behaving.

LENA   Oh, Louie: you're really something else.

LOUIE   So are you, Lena.
            (*The lights begin to come up now; we can tell that it is going to be a bright sun-filled day.* LENA *and* LOUIE *both look up at the sun and the sky. They both breath in deeply. We begin to hear the sounds of traffic now: horns honking, etcetera.* LENA *and* LOUIE *begin to walk with their shopping carts*)

LENA   Louie, let me ask you something?

LOUIE   Shoot, baby.

LENA   What do you think about us?

LOUIE   What do you mean?

LENA   What do you think about the two of us?

LOUIE   You mean about the two of us as lovers? I think there's no one like the two of us as lovers: nobody on the whole face of the earth is like the two of us when you think about the perfect subject of a pair of perfect lovers.

LENA I wasn't thinking about that. I know that's all true. I was thinking about our lives, Louie . . .

LOUIE Our lives?

LENA Yes. What are we doing with our lives? Or better still: what *aren't* we doing with our lives?

LOUIE I don't get you.

LENA Well, I don't know. I guess what I'm trying to say to you is that maybe we should think about professions, after all.

LOUIE Professions?!

LENA You know what I mean?

LOUIE I don't know what you mean at all.

LENA Then forget it.

LOUIE I will.
(LENA *stops pushing her shopping cart*)

LENA Let's stop here for awhile.

LOUIE Ah, yes! The Metropolitan Opera House . . . !

LENA The beautiful Met!
(LOUIE *stops pushing his shopping cart also*)

LOUIE (*Sitting down*) It's a nice place. It has such a nice atmosphere.

LENA (*Sitting down too*) Listen to the music.
(*We hear something from "Tosca" in the background.* LENA *and* LOUIE *listen to it*)

LENA How do you like it?

LOUIE It's okay.

LENA   Oh, Louie: it's better than just okay.

LOUIE   Well, I'm glad you think so.

LENA   But it's so peaceful.

LOUIE   But it's just not my cup of tea.

LENA   Well, I think you should force yourself to appreciate it.

LOUIE   Anything you say.
        (LENA *and* LOUIE *sit and listen to the music*)

LENA (*Finally*)   If I didn't do what I was doing with my life right now, then do you know what I would be doing?

LOUIE   What would you be doing?

LENA   I'd be hooking.

LOUIE   You mean you'd be a hooker?

LENA   That's right.

LOUIE   That's really a surprise to me.

LENA   Do you approve?

LOUIE   Do you think it would make you happy?

LENA   I think so.

LOUIE   Then I would approve.

LENA   You're so wonderful.

LOUIE   That's because you're so wonderful.

LENA   And what would you be if you weren't doing what you're doing now?

LOUIE   I'd be a politician.

LENA   Oh, I like that.

LOUIE   I'd be helping people.

LENA   That's very nice.

LOUIE   And if you were a hooker: what would you be doing for people?

LENA   I think I'd be helping them too.

LOUIE   That's also very nice.
        (*It is getting brighter and brighter outside*)

LENA   I would be a hooker, a heart-of-gold prostitute, and I would eventually fall in love with a politician about the same age as I am, but we wouldn't meet secretly, we would let the whole world know about our love affair.

LOUIE   I can buy that.

LENA   I would eventually ask you to marry me.

LOUIE   I'd ask you first.

LENA   I was hoping you would say that.

LOUIE   I would ask you to marry me first.

LENA   And I would say yes without blinking an eye-lash.

LOUIE   Would you want to have some children?

LENA   Oh, of course! Lots of them. But for the first two years I would just simply want to spend all of my time with you—in-and-out-of-bed—until we really felt that were ready to have the children, just so the children wouldn't suffer when the they grew older.

LOUIE   I like that a whole lot.

LENA   Don't you think our children would be beautiful?

LOUIE   If they took after you: they would.

LENA   And if they took after you; they would too.
(*The music from "Tosca" is beginning to fade away, and we can tell by the lighting that nighttime will soon be coming upon* LENA *and* LOUIE *again. The two of them begin to get ready for their nightly journey*)

LOUIE   It'll be dark soon.

LENA   I can hardly wait.

LOUIE   And we'll make love.

LENA   Where the Zeigfeld Theatre is . . .

LOUIE   And the Burlington Mills skyscraper . . .

LENA   And those watery little fountains.

LOUIE   I can hardly wait too.

LENA   Let's not eat tonight.

LOUIE   That's fine with me.

LENA   So we won't be wasting time.

LOUIE   Time is for love and romance: that's all it's for: and we should let the whole world know about it.

LENA   That way the whole world can from it.

LOUIE   Ah, Lena!

LENA   Ah, Louie!
(LENA *and* LOUIE *stop now. It is also dark now.* LOUIE *takes a little pack of something out of his pocket*)

LENA   Here we are. Listen to those fountains.

LOUIE   Just like another world, another time, another place.

LENA   We're so lucky, Louie.

LOUIE   Can you just imagine how lucky our kids are going to be?

LENA   Well, that's the way it should be. What's that you got in your hand, Louie?

LOUIE   (*Reading from the little pack*)   "Stimula. Manufactured by Horizon. Lubricated with SK-70. Three male contraceptive sheaths: prophylactics. Specially textured surface. Designed for her pleasure." (*He turns the pack over on the other side and goes on reading*) "Specially textured surface designed to give women more pleasure. When it's better for her . . . it's better for both. For family planning."
      (LOUIE *stops now. He looks at* LENA. *He tosses the little pack away into the immediate darkness*)

LENA   I'm so glad you threw it away. (*There is a pause*) You see this?
      (LENA *takes a little bottle of pills from out of her coat*)

LOUIE   What are those, Lena?

LENA   These are birth control pills. These pills are wonderous things and they do wonderous things inside a woman's body whenever that woman is making love. These pills prevent fear and anxiety and nervousness and hate and self-hate and wars and fighting and battles and they also prevent lying and cheating and disloyalties and, well, just about everything else that doesn't help add up to a happy life.
      (*There is another pause. And then* LENA *tosses the little bottle of pills away into the darkness nearby*)

LOUIE   It's a terrific-looking sky up there, don't you think?
      (LENA *looks up along with* LOUIE)

LENA   It's just beautiful tonight.
      (LENA *looks very lovingly at* LOUIE *who returns the same sort of look*)

LOUIE   Shall we have music?

LENA   Oh, yes . . .
      (LENA *turns on her transistor-radio. The music that we heard at the beginning of the play—Harold Melvin and*

the Blue Notes singing: "The Love I Lost"—is heard once again)

LOUIE   It's nice . . . (LENA *turns the music off*) Why did you do that for?

LENA   I don't wanna hear that music! That was the music I heard when they told about the hooker and the politician over the radio!

LOUIE   I thought you got over being superstitious.

LENA   I thought I did too.

LOUIE   It's dumb to be superstitious.

LENA   Well, I don't think so.

LOUIE   It's really dumb.

LENA   It is not!

LOUIE   It is too!

LENA   I'm getting tired!

LOUIE   Tired over what?! Tired of being superstitious again?!

LENA   I'm getting tired of our lives!

LOUIE   What does that mean?!

LENA   I'm not too sure . . . yet . . . !

LOUIE   You were never too sure: until you met me! What's got into you all of a sudden?!

LENA   I was just going to ask you the same question!

LOUIE   Yeah: well, whose gonna answer the question first?!

LENA   I'm not!

LOUIE   Yeah: that figures too!

LENA   What does that mean?!

LOUIE   It means you're back to being stubborn: just the way you're now back to being superstitious too! I feel like I've failed!

LENA   Failed over what?!

LOUIE   Failed over the fact that I got you not to be stubborn anymore, and I also got you not to be superstitious anymore! But now look at you! You're worse than ever before!

LENA   Well, we're not all perfect, are we, Louie?! That's your problem, of course: the fact that you think you're so perfect all of the time!

LOUIE   Knock it off, Lena!

LENA   Remember before: when I said I was getting tired? Well, the real reason why I said I was getting tired has to do with the plain fact that I'm getting tired over making-believe all of the time. Why did you become a bum? Why did I become a bum? We're young and good-looking and we're not that bad off up in the head? So why do we live the way we're living? I guess because it's all make-believe. We give the impression that we know all of the answers. We think that the whole world's wrong and that we're the only ones who are right. Well, I'm beginning to think that that's not true at all. I'm beginning to think that the two of us—Lena and Louie—are big phonies, and that we really been kidding ourselves, and that everyone probably thinks we're really a couple of real asshole-nothings! That's what I'm beginning to think!
   (LOUIE *tries to control himself. He does not like hearing any of this*)

LOUIE   I'm getting turned-off, Lena.

LENA   So am I, Louie.

LOUIE   Why did this all happen to us like this: all of a sudden: like this?

LENA   I guess it was supposed to happen: all of a sudden: like this.

(*The lights begin to darken a little*)

LOUIE (*After an uneasy pause*)   It looks like it's going to rain again, or something like that . . .

LENA (*After an uneasy pause*)   It really looks strange, all of a sudden: the sky up there: what a weird-looking color.
(LENA *turns her transistor-radio on*)

LOUIE   I thought you didn't want to hear any more music: especially music that was going to make you feel superstitious all over again?

LENA   I want the weather report.

RADIO ANNOUNCER (*Over the radio*)   An icy cold ice wave is suddenly due to hit the Metropolitan area sometime late tonight. It is going to go below freezing. Some experts predict that it will set an all-time record, especially for this time of the year. One expert flatly predicts that the temperature will go down to seventeen degrees below zero sometime tonight. And the wind will be wild and furious and freezing . . .
(LENA *turns off her transistor-radio*)

LOUIE   Well, you certainly got it, didn't you?

LENA   I certainly got what?

LOUIE   The weather report.

LENA   Yes, it's really something, isn't it?

LOUIE   I'll bet you never counted on hearing what we both just heard, did you?

LENA   I wonder what it means.

LOUIE   It means exactly what you heard.

LENA   It's got to mean more than that.

LOUIE   Well, forget about it: because it doesn't!

LENA   There you go again, Louie: raising your voice at me!

LOUIE That's what you're doing too!
(*We hear the first sounds of the wind*)

LENA Did you hear it?

LOUIE It's the wind. Big deal.

LENA Where shall we go?

LOUIE When?

LENA Tonight.

LOUIE You mean because of the weather?

LENA Yes.

LOUIE I think we should go to Sheep's Meadow in Central Park, that's where I think we should go.

LENA You must be crazy. We'll never last in all of that open space.

LOUIE Who knows? We might. We're strong. We're both used to being outdoors. Why not? It's just as good as any other place, when you really think about it.

LENA I still think you're crazy, Louie.

LOUIE Happy-crazy, Lena, happy-crazy.

LENA Well, I guess I am too, if you are too: happy-crazy. (*The wind howls in the background again*) Oh, dear: just listen to it: the howling wind . . .

LOUIE The howling wind: wild and furious and freezing! It's sort of turning me on, Lena.

LENA You're crazy, Louie.

LOUIE *Happy*-crazy!

LENA *Happy*-crazy then.

(LOUIE *begins to push his shopping cart, and so,* LENA *follows after him*)

LOUIE　　Turn you're radio back on.

LENA　　Okay.
(LENA *turns her transistor-radio back on. We hear O.C. Smith singing: "Could It Be I'm Falling In Love."* LOUIE *and* LENA *begin to move their bodies with the music as they also continue on with the pushing of their shopping carts. Then, suddenly,* LOUIE *stops in his tracks, and so,* LENA *stops in her tracks as well*)

LOUIE　　Shit, Lena.

LENA　　What's the matter?

LOUIE　　(*Facing her*)　We think we know all of the answers, honey. We gotta start taking more chances in our lives. We're too mellowed. We gotta start sticking our heads into things more often. We're wasting our lives so long as we play it so goddam safe all of the time. Do you know what I'm getting at, honey? I'm getting at the fact that we're really a pair of lovers who are really pretty ordinary, who ain't really got much passion going for them. What's that word, that word that means it has something to do without much sex going for it? What's the word, Lena? *Asexual* . . . ! I mean: just look what we have to do? We have to pretend that we're somebody else all of the time. I never call you Lena when we're making love, and you never call me Louie, either. I'm calling you Jackie or Gloria or Elizabeth and a million other names of famous ladies, and you're always calling me Marcello or Marlon or Warren and a million other names of famous men. Do you know what I'm saying, honey? I want to call you Lena when we're making love together and I want you to call me Louie when we're making love together, if you know what I mean, honey.

LENA　　I know what you mean, darling, and it really makes me happy that you're thinking the way you're thinking all of a sudden like this.

LOUIE　　Let's go then.

LENA　　Where to?

LOUIE   To the middle of Sheep's Meadow in the middle of Central Park.
(LOUIE and LENA begin to push their shopping-carts side-by-side now. The sky is getting darker now)

LOUIE   Shall we have some music?

LENA   Oh, yes . . .
(LENA turns on her transistor-radio again. We hear: Diana Ross and Marvin Gaye singing together: "Include Me In Your Life")

LENA   Oh, I love this song: "Include Me In Your Life."

LOUIE   It's a pretty nice title for a song, don't you think, Lena.

LENA   Yeah: for someone like you and me. Louie.
(The music is interrupted by a RADIO ANNOUNCER)

RADIO ANNOUNCER   We're sorry to interrupt this program but . . .

LOUIE   Yeah! We're sorry too!

RADIO ANNOUNCER   But . . . the double funeral of the two ill-fated lovers, the dashing young politician and the dazzling young prostitute, Rico and Rusty, or, Rusty and Rico, took place very quietly and very quickly late this afternoon out in Queens somewhere, since there was no next of kin and no children and no other remaining survivors.
(The music comes back on again. LENA and LOUIE are very serene now as they continue to head on towards Central Park)

LENA   I'm glad that it was a double funeral.

LOUIE   I am too.

LENA   I'm so glad they were together.

LOUIE   So am I.
(They now both approach The Tavern-On-The-Green in Central Park)

LENA   This is terrible, Louie . . . !
          (LENA *looks up at all of the dark trees around the place*)

LOUIE   Listen, Lena: I gotta go to the bathroom fast! It's a bad
          case of number one!

LENA   Oh, it's terrible! All of the lights are off in all of the
          trees . . . !
          (LOUIE *runs behind a bunch of high bushes*)

LOUIE (*Sighing*) Oh, Lena . . . thank God . . . what a plea-
          sure . . . I thought I was going to bust before, Lena . . . !

LENA   I want those lights back on . . . they were so pretty,
          Louie.
          (LOUIE *lets out a loud yelp*)

LENA   What's the matter, Louie?!

LOUIE   I tripped on something, that's all. Hey, wait a minute,
          Lena? Do you know what it is?! It's a light socket.

LENA   A light socket . . . ?

LOUIE   Yeah, and the plug is out. Maybe I should plug it back in
          and we'll see what happens.
          (LOUIE *plugs the socket together again; all of the lights in
          all of the trees come back on*)

LENA   Oh, Louie! You can do anything!

LOUIE (*Coming from the bushes*) Jesus, Lena: I feel like a
          miracle-man, or something like that.
          (LENA *kisses* LOUIE *as they both look up at all of the
          twinkling lights in all of the trees*)
          (LENA *and* LOUIE *go off into the darkness now with their
          shopping carts as it becomes strangely darker and we hear
          the howling wind once again, along with the music from
          the transistor-radio. Presently,* LENA *and* LOUIE *appear
          again: they are in Sheep's Meadow now*)

LOUIE   Here we are! In the middle of Sheep's Meadow in the
          middle of Central Park! My favorite place in the whole
          world . . .

LENA   Mine too! It makes me think that were both on top of the world somewhere.

>   (*The wind is heard again. The lights flicker. The darkness goes into an orange-color. It is rather chilling, but it is also rather beautiful in a strange sort of way*)

LOUIE   You know something? We gotta be like them.

LENA   You mean Rusty and Rico?

LOUIE   Yes. We gotta be like them. That was real and it was full of passion. They didn't have any hang-ups. They just had real true honest passionate love going between them, that's all!

LENA   That's all there is. There isn't anything more.

LOUIE   How do you feel?

LENA   I'm feeling a little chilly.

LOUIE   Don't let it bother you.

LENA   I'll try not to.

LOUIE   Everything's going to be okay.

LENA   I'm taking your word for it.

LOUIE   This is our place, honey. This is our world.

LENA   Feel that air. It's beginning to freeze.

LOUIE   Better to freeze than to melt.

LENA   I never thought of it that way: better to freeze than to melt. I like that. It's a nice thought. To be frozen forever, always preserved, forever, never ever really gone, forever, always around, forever, still existing, no matter what, forever, reminding people that you didn't disappear, forever, making the world never forget you, forever, always totally eternal, forever, and ever and ever!

LOUIE   You got the idea.

LENA   Melting away is horrible. You just simply disappear when
you melt away.

LOUIE   Like I said before: better to be frozen than to be melted.
(LENA *begins to rummage through her shopping cart*) What are
you looking for?

LENA   Wine.

LENA   Yes, wine.

LOUIE   Whose wine?

LENA   My grandfather's wine.
(LENA *continues to search through her shopping cart*)

LOUIE   Your grandfather's wine?

LENA   Yes, my grandfather's wine on my mother's side: my
mother's father: my other grandfather.

LOUIE   But he's dead, isn't he?

LENA   Yes, he is.

LOUIE   You told me he died years ago, your grandfather on your
mother's side.

LENA   That's right: he did: over thirteen years ago: on the exact
same night before I was going to my first prom when I was still
in high school.

LOUIE   It must be old wine then: if he gave it to you.
(LENA *finds the bottle of red wine*)

LENA   Oh, here it is! My Grandfather Fedelio's homemade red
Italian wine that he made all by himself here in America, over
on Long Island somewhere, where he grew his own red grapes
himself. This ruby red wine is over thirteen years old, Louie,
and my Grandfather Fedelio gave it to me right before he died
the night before my first prom night, but because he died that
night before, well, I decided not to drink it, I decided to keep it

for a night like tonight, and I never went to the prom, after all, because of my Grandfather Fedelio's dying away, all of a sudden, like he did. I loved him so much! And it'll be good for us, this special red wine, going through our bodies, through our muscles and veins and through our blood, building up our blood, and keeping it warm and hot and flowing and making it even more red than it already is! Thank you, Grandfather Fedelio, wherever you are!

(LENA *opens up the bottle of red wine*)

LOUIE Grandfather Fedelio? What kind of name is that?

LENA *Fedelio* means: *faithful.*

LOUIE That's nice: *faithful.*

LENA And, oh my God! Did he ever live up to his name! And, oh my God! Did it ever rub off on the rest of us! And do you know what, Louie? Right away it makes me think of that prostitute and that politician . . .

LOUIE Rusty and Rico . . .

LENA Yes . . . Rusty and Rico . . . they were really and truly faithful!

LOUIE Like maybe: we should be really and truly faithful to them: Rusty and Rico.

LENA Of course, Louie.
(LENA *offers the bottle of red wine to* LOUIE)

LENA Here: take a big sip.
(LOUIE *takes the bottle of red wine*)

LOUIE Thank you, I will.
(LOUIE *takes a big sip of the red wine from the bottle*)

LENA How is it?

LOUIE Wonderful! Really wonderful!
(LOUIE *hands the bottle to* LENA; *she takes a big sip of the red wine from the bottle now*)

LOUIE   So what do you think?

LENA   I think it's better than that Rothschild stuff from Lutece.

LOUIE   I was thinking the same thing.
(LOUIE *drinks some more*)

LENA   I love it here, Pussycat. Just look at all those lights in the twinkling windows of all those towers of all those skyscrapers! All around us: on all four sides! It's just like a sort of Utopia—I think that's the right word: Utopia—all of those windows with all of those people behind all of those windows: living and breathing and trying to love too! Well, I just love it all, my dear Louie Pussycat! All of them trying like holy hell and holy heaven to be wholly holy happy as much as it's humanly possible in all of our rather only half-happy lives, instead of our wholly happy holy lives . . . !
(LOUIE *passes the bottle of red wine to* LENA; *she drinks from it*)

LOUIE   I feel like we're Adam and Eve out here. I feel that we're really doing the right thing by being out here. Despite the warnings of the coming freezing storm. I feel that it's really and truly better to be out here than to be inside somewhere, taking shelter, hiding from it all, if you know what I mean, precious Lena. We're both out here because, well, we were born out here, for all time, like everybody else was born out here, outside, for all time.
(*The wind howls furiously now. It is rather frightening.* LENA *goes to* LOUIE. *He takes her in his arms. They hold onto each other for a long time while the wind rushes in-and-around them, practically drowning out anything that could otherwise be heard in Sheep's Meadow*)

LOUIE   We're gonna make love, Sophia.

LENA   My name is Lena.

LOUIE   I'm sorry . . . Lena. Lena?

LENA   Yes, Rudolph . . . ?

LOUIE   My name is Louie.

LENA   I apologize, Louie.

LOUIE   Lena?

LENA   Yes, Louie.

LOUIE   We're gonna make love, Lena.

LENA   That makes me so happy, Louie.
(*The wind becomes worse. It howls like a violent unseen "thing."* LOUIE *and* LENA *slowly begin to freeze in each other's arms. The lights begin to flicker on-and-off*)

LOUIE   My . . . love . . . for YOU!

LENA   Yes, YES!
(LENA *and* LOUIE *are shouting above the wind now*)

LOUIE   My . . . LOVE FOR YOU AIN'T CHANGING! IT'S GROWING!

LENA   GROWING! YES! FOREVER IT'S GROWING! FOREVER!
(*Now there is a huge blast of howling wind; it is catastrophic; one can almost feel that the roof of the theatre could even be blown off all of a sudden. The lights flicker crazily, everywhere. And the wind grows and grows and grows. And* LENA *and* LOUIE *freeze and freeze and freeze: in each other's freezing hot arms*)

LOUIE   Lena . . . !

LENA   Louie . . . !

LOUIE   I LOVE YOU!

LENA   AND I LOVE YOU!

LOUIE   FOREVER!

LENA   AND EVER AND EVER AND EVER!
(*The wind truly drowns their voices out now. But we can somehow manage to hear* LENA *say her last few words*)

LENA OH, GOD, GOD, GOD!

(LENA *and* LOUIE *are now totally frozen to death—and life—in each other's frozen arms. Eventually the howling violent wind dies away. Before we all know it: there is complete, utterly total silence. The serenity is quite beautiful to behold Utter silence. Tableau: the frozen* LENA *and* LOUIE, *like two rare and precious marble statues famous throughout the world for their uniqueness and their sheer beauty. Finally, we hear a* RADIO ANNOUNCER *coming from somewhere. It is the* VOICE *of a man at first)*

RADIO ANNOUNCER It was the most bitter and the most violent wind-storm since the beginning of time. Thousands of lives have been lost, taken away by the angry wind, the howling and furious wind! It will take years to determine the damage, but it will take *forever* to determine who was lost . . . and, perhaps: why? Why?!

(*The* RADIO ANNOUNCER'S VOICE *is now that of a bright and very cheerful-sounding young woman)*

RADIO ANNOUNCER In Central Park, right smack in the middle of Sheep's Meadow, wide-open to all of the endless elements of nature—and, perhaps: God too—a young and beautiful couple, whose first names were Lena and Louie, were found frozen to death, standing up, in each other's arms, with the two most beautiful smiles on their faces: smiling like one has never seen smiling, ever before in one's rather minute and passing life, smiling smiles that told of things like, well, things like . . . *forever!*

(*We continue to gaze at the frozen "double statue" of* LENA *and* LOUIE, *smiling, in each other's arms, while not a single sound is heard now. There is utter peace in the theatre now)*

A SLOW DIMOUT

The End

ABOUT THE AUTHOR

Leonard Melfi was born and educated in Binghamton, New York, and attended St. Bonaventure University, the American Academy of Dramatic Arts, and the Uta Hagen-Herbert Berghof Studios.

After spending two years in Europe in the U.S. Army, Mr. Melfi came to New York City determined to be an actor. Abandoning this profession, he wrote poetry for a year, had two poems published, and then began to write plays. His plays have been produced on Broadway, Off-Broadway, Off-Off-Broadway, and all over the world, from Cafe LaMama to The Circle-in-the-Square in New York, to The Mark Taper Forum in Los Angeles, and the Royal Court of London, among the numerous other places. Among many organizations he is a member of The Dramatists Guild and The Eugene O'Neill Memorial Theatre Foundation.

His plays have also appeared on national television as well as on the B.B.C. of Great Britain, and he wrote the film, *Lady Liberty,* especially for Sophia Loren.

He was awarded two consecutive Rockefeller Foundation Grants for play writing in 1967 and 1968, and in 1978 he won a Guggenheim Fellowship for his play writing.

His *Notes of a New York Playwright* appear in each issue of The Dramatists Guild quarterly. He makes his home in New York City.